BACKROAD BICYCLING
in Connecticut

White's Woods in Litchfield.

BACKROAD BICYCLING
in Connecticut

32 Scenic Rides on Country Lanes and Dirt Roads

Andi Marie Fusco

Backcountry Guides
Woodstock · Vermont

With time, road numbers, signs, park regulations, and amenities may change. If you find that such changes have occurred along the routes described in this book, please let the author and publisher know so that corrections may be made in future editions. Other comments and suggestions are also welcome. Address all correspondence to:

Editor, Backroad Bicycle Tours
Backcountry Guides
P.O. Box 748
Woodstock, VT 05091

Library of Congress Cataloging-in-Publication Data
Fusco, Andi Marie, 1969–
Backroad bicycling in Connecticut : 32 scenic rides on country lanes and dirt roads / Andi Marie Fusco.
        p. cm.
   ISBN 0-88150-438-6 (alk. paper)
   1. Bicycle touring—Connecticut—Guidebooks. 2. Connecticut—Guidebooks. I. Title.
GV1045.5.C66 F87 2000
917.4604'43—dc21

                                          99–058148

Cover design by Joanna Bodenweber
Text design by Sally Sherman
Cover photograph by Jack Affleck/Index Stock Photography
Interior photographs by Andi Marie Fusco
Maps by Paul Woodward, © 2000 The Countryman Press
Published by The Countryman Press, P.O. Box 748, Woodstock, Vermont 05091
Distributed by W. W. Norton & Company, Inc., 500 Fifth Avenue, New York, NY 10110
Printed in the United States of America
10 9 8 7 6 5 4 3 2

For V. J. Fusco

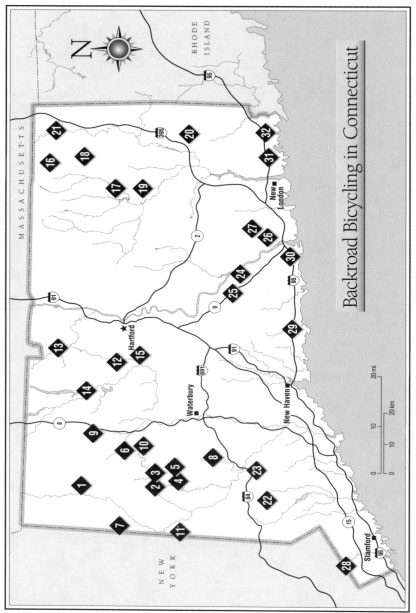

Backroad Bicycling in Connecticut

Paul Woodward, © 2000 The Countryman Press

Contents

Acknowledgments

I would like to recognize all the people whose knowledge, advice, and support made this book possible.

Special thanks go to Greg Martin, Suzette Andrade, Paula Signora, Felicia Jarosz, and others who accompanied me on the rides, often enduring long treks across the state and waiting patiently while I scribbled notes at each junction and point of interest along the route.

I am also grateful to the many bike shops that were generous with their advice and route ideas, especially Jim Abbott and Jenn Brown at Cycle Loft in Litchfield, Fran Moniz and Jason Langlois at Silver Bicycle Co. in Putnam, Scott Johnson at Scott's Cyclery in Willimantic, Clarke White at Clarke Cycles in Essex, Rob Kapell at Mystic Cycle Center in Mystic, Dave Cope at Buzz's Cycles in Old Greenwich, Brian Cohen at Central Wheel in West Hartford, and Peter Piepul at Valley Bicycle in Granby.

Thanks also to Georgette Yaindl, executive director of the Connecticut Bike Coalition, for her input and enthusiasm; Brian Smith, president of the Connecticut chapter of the New England Mountain Bike Association (NEMBA), for assistance on the West Hartford Reservoir route; Todd Rosenthal for providing contacts in the bicycling community; John Murray for his photography advice; Florence Minor for her wisdom; and Brian and Amy Cantele, Brigitte Ruthman, Peter Serratore, and Nancy Rosette for their ride ideas.

Finally, I am grateful to Helen Whybrow, Ann Kraybill, and Jennifer Goneau at Backcountry Guides for their guidance; and to my family for their neverending encouragement.

All of you helped make this book possible.

Backroad Bicycle Tours at a Glance

Ride	Region	Distance
1. Covered Bridge to Lime Rock	Litchfield Hills	16.2
2. New Preston to Bulls Bridge	Litchfield Hills	30.0
3. Lake Waramaug	Litchfield Hills	8.7
4. Washington Depot to Bethlehem	Litchfield Hills	23.8
5. Steep Rock Reservation	Litchfield Hills	14.0
6. Litchfield to Norfolk	Litchfield Hills	47.9
7. Macedonia to the Twin Lakes	Litchfield Hills	50.8
8. The Litchfield Hills	Litchfield Hills	114.6
9. Winchester Center to Norfolk	Litchfield Hills	44.2
10. White's Woods	Litchfield Hills	8.9
11. Gaylordsville to Sherman	Litchfield Hills	16.8
12. Winding Trails	North Country	12.0
13. Salmon Brook to New-Gate	North Country	28.5
14. Farmington River Roads	North Country	25.2
15. West Hartford Reservoir	North Country	8.2
16. Woodstock: Dairy Country	Quiet Corner	14.8
17. Goodwin & Natchaug Forests	Quiet Corner	15.4
18. Pomfret to Brooklyn	Quiet Corner	17.8

Difficulty	Bike	Kids?	Highlights
Moderate	Road	NO	A rural dirt road along the Housatonic
Strenuous	Road	NO	A historic covered bridge
Easy	Road	YES	A pleasant loop around a spectacular lake
Moderate to Strenuous	Road	NO	Historic homes and farmland
Moderate	Mtn.	NO	A beautiful hidden agricultural valley
Strenuous	Road	NO	Rural Colonial villages
Moderate to Strenuous	Hybrid	NO	Miles of hidden dirt roads
Strenuous	Road	NO	A scenic tour of pastoral northwest Connecticut
Strenuous	Road	NO	Rural woods and village greens
Moderate	Mtn.	YES	Marshes, streams, and forest in a wildlife preserve
Moderate	Road	NO	Ride past a preserved 19th-century railroad hotel
Easy	Mtn.	YES	Great family off-road riding
Moderate	Road	NO	Historic copper mine and prison
Moderate to Strenuous	Road	NO	A scenic stretch of the Farmington River
Moderate	Mtn.	YES	Rugged terrain close to Hartford
Moderate	Road	NO	Hills dotted with dairy farms
Easy	Mtn.	YES	A scenic rail trail through two state forests
Moderate	Road	NO	Ride through a National Heritage Corridor

Ride	Region	Distance
19. Windham to Lebanon	Quiet Corner	48.0/61.3
20. Pachaug State Forest	Quiet Corner	8.8
21. The Thompson Green	Quiet Corner	7.5
22. Collis P. Huntington State Park	River Valleys	4.5+
23. Newtown to Weir Farm	River Valleys	41.0
24. Chester to Killingworth	River Valleys	39.3
25. Cockaponset State Forest	River Valleys	10.0/20.0
26. Connecticut River Crossings	River Valleys	25.0/40.5
27. Lyme/Old Lyme	River Valleys	27.0/37.0
28. Greenwich: The Backcountry	Shoreline	21.9
29. The Thimble Islands	Shoreline	19.1
30. Old Saybrook: Shore Points	Shoreline	8.9
31. Bluff Point State Park and Coastal Reserve	Shoreline	4.0
32. Stonington	Shoreline	28.9

Difficulty	Bike	Kids?	Highlights
Strenuous	Road	NO	Picturesque New England villages
Moderate	Mtn.	YES	Connecticut's largest forest
Moderate	Road	NO	A charming hilltop village green
Moderate	Mtn.	YES	Meandering trails through rocky terrain
Strenuous	Road	NO	Connecticut's only National Historic Site
Moderate	Road	NO	Rural roads through the Connecticut River Valley
Moderate	Mtn.	NO	Thickly wooded dirt roads and trails
Strenuous	Road	NO	Cross the Connecticut River on a 17th-century ferry service
Moderate to Strenuous	Road	NO	Panoramic views of Hamburg Cove
Strenuous	Road	NO	Genteel country estates
Easy	Road	NO	A charming seaside village
Easy	Road	YES	An easy and scenic ride that hugs the shoreline
Moderate	Mtn.	YES	A sandy bluff overlooking Long Island Sound
Moderate	Road	NO	A well-preserved 19th-century fishing village

Introduction

May all your trails be crooked, winding, lonesome, leading to the most amazing view—where something as strange and more beautiful and more full of wonder than your deepest dreams waits for you.

—Edward Abbey

Despite its diminutive size, Connecticut's landscape is blessed with a wealth of diversity, which surprises many first-time visitors and makes for memorable cycling. It is truly part of New England and has all the character and beauty of its neighboring states to the north, from the densely forested peaks in the western highlands and green-clad hills in the northeast, the long low fertile river valleys, and a 250-mile craggy shoreline along Long Island Sound. The state is sliced in two by its namesake river—New England's longest—410 miles from the headwaters in northern New Hampshire to its mouth near Old Saybrook.

Connecticut is a compact state; at a mere 5,000 square miles it's the country's third smallest, larger only than Rhode Island and Delaware. It's 90 miles east to west, 55 miles from Long Island Sound to the Massachusetts border, making no spot in the state more than a 2-hour drive from any other. This small scale makes it easy to get around; it's feasible to plan a morning ride in the northwestern Litchfield Hills and tour the southeast coastline later in the day.

Outside of the pockets of urban sprawl, there exists a vast number of scenic, lightly traveled back roads and trails for cyclists who are willing to venture off the beaten path and find them. Countryside that rolls by like a silent film to motorists comes to life with the sound of birds and farm tractors and the scent of autumn leaves and rain.

The pleasure of riding in Connecticut is in the quintessential New England scenes at every turn. Litchfield's picture-postcard 18th-century green, covered bridges spanning the Housatonic River, grand sea captains' homes in maritime villages like Essex and Stonington, and the colonial order of the white clapboard homes on Washington's lovely hilltop green are among the images giving way to rolling hills of fields and forest.

I've divided the state into five regions: the rugged Litchfield Hills; the rolling North Country area above Hartford; the bucolic Quiet Corner that includes Woodstock and Brooklyn; the historic sites and villages in the Housatonic and Connecticut River Valleys; and the intricate shoreline from Greenwich to Stonington. Each region has a distinct geography and flavor.

The Litchfield Hills, in the northwest corner, is one of the most photographed, written about, and painted regions of state. It embodies all that is classic New England, from its quaint inns and colonial meeting-houses to the barns and silos dotting the rugged hills. Hidden dirt roads and meandering country lanes fan across the area, making it a cycling mecca. The foothills of the Berkshires march across here, so the climbs are challenging, the descents often hair-raising.

The North Country is an attractive mix of rolling hills and fertile plains along the Connecticut River, where the roads are lined with produce stands and tobacco is still a major agricultural crop. Despite its proximity to Hartford's sprawling suburbs, one can find forested hills and tranquil country roads along the banks of the Farmington River.

The rural northeast corner, also known as the Quiet Corner, is blanketed with meadows, orchards, farm fields, and thick woodlands. It's part of the Quinebaug and Shetucket Rivers Valley National Heritage Corridor, an 850-square-mile region considered the "last green valley" in the Boston-to-Washington, D.C., megalopolis. You'll ride through pristine enclaves like Thompson, Woodstock, and Pomfret, which pride themselves on their 18th-century appearance. Pachaug State Forest is arguably the state's wildest, most unspoiled natural area; at 30,000 acres it's by all accounts the largest.

Storybook villages strung along the Connecticut River retain the flavor of long-ago seafaring days. Artists, vacationers and retirees flock to Essex, whose elegant architecture and maritime museum reflect the whaling and trading industries on which the village was founded centuries ago. The river referred to in the 1960s as "one of the nation's best landscaped sewers" is now on The Nature Conservancy's list of "100 Last Great Places," home to a thriving population of herons, ospreys, and bald

Cycling past a Colonial home in Salem.

eagles. The lower Housatonic River cuts a swath through suburbia but has large tracts of preserved open space and quiet, scenic roads.

Along the shoreline of Long Island Sound, Stonington, Old Saybrook, and Mystic prospered in the maritime trade of the 18th and 19th centuries. In the 1800s, more ships were built in Mystic than in any other town in the nation. Today, its majestic tall ships, aquarium, and re-created 19th-century whaling village are Connecticut's number-one tourist attractions.

One of New England's most indelible images is of the town green, the neat grassy rectangle presided over by soaring church spires and antique homes and perhaps a general store or grange hall. Along Connecticut's back roads, these greens look similar to when they were laid out in the 17th and 18th centuries. The best ones, like in Thompson, Sharon, Lebanon, and Woodstock, have to be sought out, and those that find them are rewarded with a close look at a vestige of New England's past. Many of these tours pass by them.

Pedaling along Connecticut's back roads, one can't help but notice the rambling stone walls crisscrossing meadows and woods, a nod to the perseverance of 17th-century colonists who carved out a living in the harsh New England soil. Today, much of that farmland is second- and third-growth forest of oak, maple, and hickory. Sometimes only the rubble of a timeworn stone wall bears witness to the existence of a farm. Connecticut's woodlands are now flourishing after two centuries of heavy farming and logging, which ebbed after the Industrial Revolution lured many Connecticut farmers away from the plow. Today more than 200,000 acres are protected as state parks and forests. As a result, wildlife is making a swift comeback. If you ride in the early morning hours or around dusk, especially by streams, ponds, or other water sources, you will likely see some of the resident wildlife, which includes deer, wild turkeys, osprey, hawks, coyote, and even the elusive black bear and bobcat.

Connecticut's forests are laced with hundreds of miles of trails, retired logging roads, and cross-country ski trails awaiting riders of all abilities. Many of these paths are blissfully solitary; you may ride all day and see few other souls. Bikes are not allowed on the Appalachian Trail or on the state's 500-mile network of blue-blazed trails; however, individual parks or private land trusts have the option of opening sections of these trails to cyclists.

Cycling is a four-season activity in Connecticut. In spring, the hills are cloaked in delicate shades of green, and wildflowers bloom beside back roads as the countryside comes back to life, with farmers plowing fields and rivers rushing with snowmelt. Riding along the coast and through dark forests is a pleasure in summer. Autumn's crisp warm days and cool nights make for spectacular foliage displays that rival any in New England; brilliant crimson sugar maples, deep green hemlocks, and bright golden hickories all combine to create a fiery tapestry. Country inns and B&Bs book months in advance during peak foliage season, which centers around the first three weeks in October. Winters can be surprisingly mild for New England, making bicycling possible year-round.

When pedaling around the state, keep in mind that Connecticut figures prominently in cycling history. The first patent for a complete bicycle was issued to Connecticut resident and mechanic Pierre Lallement in 1866. His machine, equipped with wooden wheels and iron tires, was aptly dubbed the "bone shaker." The patent was later purchased by Albert Pope, and by 1878 Pope's Hartford company produced the first high-wheeled Columbia bicycles and set off a national craze that lasted through the turn of the 20th century. (Columbia continued mass-pro-ducing bikes until 1991.) These first bicycles inspired fantasies of speed and freedom while drawing riders away from their everyday lives; the appeal is much the same for today's cyclists.

About the Rides

This book is your guide to all kinds of rides across Connecticut. Some will challenge riders on hills replete with lung-searing climbs through the state's highest elevations that make the end seem earned. Others will appeal to those who want to take an unhurried tour around a lake or along hidden dirt roads, stopping to picnic, swim, or just savor the journey. Some visit Connecticut's earliest colonial settlements and pass by the state's renowned wineries, and still others explore the woodlands on trails.

Distances range from a 4-mile trail through a coastal reserve to a 2-day tour of 114 miles.

Each ride is designed to be completed in a day—sometimes in a morning or afternoon, except for the 2-day Litchfield Hills tour and a strenuous ride in the Quiet Corner that offers cyclists the option of stretching it into a couple of easy days.

Each tour is described thoroughly so you can easily judge which ones suit your interest and ability. Information is provided on distance, terrain, area bicycle shops and lodging options (for the overnight tours), as well as detailed route descriptions. A note on mileage: Keep in mind that each bike computer is calibrated differently, therefore the mileage in the ride descriptions may vary from your own calculations. Your best bet is to use a bike computer and pay attention to signposts and landmarks to keep you on the right path.

Local bike shops are among a cyclist's best resources, a place to get supplies or repairs as well as information on group rides or local cycling events. See which ones are close to the route you choose and stop by before heading out on a ride.

The Terrain

Connecticut's landscape of shoreline, valleys, and mountains make for diverse riding conditions, whether you're road riding or out on a trail. The most challenging riding is not, as one might expect, relegated to the eastern and western uplands. The southwest corner of the state is flush with tight, compact ridges that have climbs that are brutish, but shorter than the ones farther north. The lowland river valleys offer flat stretches laced with winding country roads, and beach roads are perfect for an easy ride along the coast.

Off-road terrain ranges from cross-country ski trails and gated dirt roads to miles of rugged singletrack trails offering a more challenging way to explore the woods. Most of the off-road routes in this book focus on easy to moderate trails, with options available for those interested in more technical riding.

When enjoying these rides, it's wise to remember a truism regarding rural country roads: They are often narrow, winding, without a shoulder for cyclists to ride on, and used by motorists who may be unaccustomed to sharing the road with cyclists. Use appropriate caution and ride responsibly and defensively.

Bicycle Safety

Road Riding

Wear a helmet. Connecticut state law requires children under 16 to wear one. Besides dramatically decreasing the risk of a head injury—by 85 percent, according to the Bicycling Helmet Safety Institute—a helmet will also shield your head from sun and cold. The side straps should be taut and the helmet level and low on your forehead when the chin strap is fastened. Try to push your helmet up from front and back. If it moves more than an inch, the straps are too loose.

Make yourself as visible as possible to motorists, pedestrians, and other cyclists by wearing bright clothing (reflectors and a bike light are also a good idea if riding at dusk). Ride predictably and in the same direction as traffic, yet always assume that a motorist cannot see you.

Always be prepared for the unexpected. When riding past parked cars, expect a door to open. Be on the lookout for oncoming cars turning left in front of you, cars pulling into traffic, or drivers passing and then making a right turn in front of you. Watch out for hazards in the road; don't brake or turn suddenly on slippery or loose surfaces such as wet leaves, manhole covers, sand, or gravel. Be especially careful when crossing railroad tracks.

Remember that motorists have a lot to pay attention to, so do your best to help avoid problems or accidents. Motorists and cyclists should not ignore each other; use clear hand signals so drivers know where you're going. Ride defensively by establishing eye contact with motorists when possible to ensure they see you, to reinforce your intentions, and to determine theirs—don't rely on a turn signal.

Most car/bike accidents occur at or near intersections. Cyclists must ride with the flow of traffic to the right; if too far to the right, cars will overtake you and cut you off. As you approach the intersection, merge with traffic. If you're not comfortable doing this, or if the intersection is too busy, get off your bike and cross on foot.

On back roads, you're likely to encounter the occasional loose and unpredictable dog. Some are just curious or may want to play, others might attack. Ignore them if they're far away; if you're approached, keep pedaling or squirt it with your water bottle. If you decide to stop, talk to it in a firm voice and keep your bike between you and the dog.

Off-Road Riding

It's every cyclist's responsibility to ride safely and considerately and be educated on the universal rules of trail etiquette. Respecting the trail will result in fewer trail closures, thereby increasing mountain biking opportunities for everyone. Remember, people will judge all cyclists by your actions.

In spring, avoid riding on muddy trails or during or after rain, which will cause serious trail damage and accelerate erosion. Respect temporary trail closures that often follow a long winter of snow and rain, which makes trails fragile; bicycles may also be prohibited from trails due to nesting birds or other wildlife activity. Heed signs that warn of private property or requirements for permits.

Take the time to do trail maintenance. Something as simple as moving fallen branches off a trail will keep others from riding around them and furthering erosion.

You will be sharing the trail with hikers and other users. Often people on foot don't even hear a bike until it's right behind them. Make them aware of your presence, and slow your pace as you pass. Enter a turn or other blind spot with the expectation that someone is around the bend.

Horses often spook easily and might be startled by your bicycle. When approaching equestrians, dismount and stand quietly until the horses pass. If approaching from behind, call out to the rider well in advance so they can stop and let you by. Leave as much room as possible before passing.

Be self-sufficient at all times: Don't rely on others for water, food, tools, or trail knowledge. Carry necessary supplies and be knowledgeable of the weather, your ability, and the area in which you're riding. If riding alone, let someone know where you are going and how long you plan to be out.

Use extra caution when mountain biking during hunting season if you are in an area that allows it; in Connecticut this includes some state forests and private wildlife management areas. Peak hunting activity is from early October through December; early morning hours are the most popular hunting times, especially on Saturday and holidays. Hunting is not permitted in Connecticut on Sunday. Wear bright colors when biking in hunting areas, and if you see someone hunting, call out so they know you're there. For more information, contact the Department of Environmental Protection Wildlife Division at 860-424-3011.

IMBA Rules of the Trail

The International Mountain Bicycling Association has developed the following trail use guidelines:

1. Ride on open (legal) trails only.
2. Leave no trace. (Whatever you had when you arrived is what you leave with.)
3. Control your bicycle.
4. Always yield trails. (Yield right-of-way to hikers, equestrians, and slower cyclists, and make them aware of your presence well in advance when approaching from behind.)
5. Never spook animals.
6. Plan ahead.

Helpful Hints

Plan ahead as much as possible. Check the map before you leave, as well as the weather forecast. Keep in mind that seasonal conditions may make a ride longer than usual. Knowing how to change or repair a flat tire can mean the difference between a minor delay and a bringing a great ride to a sound halt.

Keeping your bike well maintained is important to how it performs on a ride. Get into the habit of bringing it to a bike shop each spring for a full tune-up.

Before a ride, you (or a bike mechanic) should inspect your bike for the following:

- Check tire pressure, tread, and sidewalls for wear.
- Check brakes and brake pads, and make sure the pads aren't rubbing against the rims. Also be sure brake cables aren't frayed; the brake lever should not touch the handlebars when squeezed.
- Spray lubricant on a squeaky chain.
- Spin your wheels; check that the wheel rotates evenly and doesn't rub against the brake pads.
- Check the saddle and handlebars. Neither should twist if pulled on. If they're loose, tighten them.

Riding Tips

Thanks to the virtually nonexistent learning curve, most people can pick up a bike and ride. From there, you can go from staying upright and pedaling to polishing your technique to get even more out of cycling.

When pedaling, don't just push down on the pedals; instead, visualize "pedaling circles." Pedal through the stroke by pushing forward with one foot at the top of the chain ring while pulling up with the other foot (imagine scraping gum or wiping mud off your shoe). Work on developing a smooth, fast pedaling motion as opposed to being a "push-push" rider. You'll use different muscle groups and won't tire as easily as a result.

For many riders, climbing is the most difficult part of cycling. The mistake many beginners make is to ambitiously tackle a hill only to run out of gas halfway up. When approaching a long climb, choose a gear that will allow you to maintain a steady, sustainable pace. Try alternating seated climbing with short periods of standing to work different muscles and rest the ones that are starting to fatigue. If it's a short hill, get out of the saddle and sprint over.

On steep off-road trails, bend at the elbows and lean your chest forward toward the top tube; this will keep your front wheel on the ground.

Try installing bar-ends to your handlebars; this will force your weight to shift forward and help keep the front tire weighed down.

Planning is key to staying in control when stopping quickly. When approaching a sharp corner, brake before the turn, then release the front brake and use the rear brake. If you enter a turn too fast, tap the rear brake. If riding across a slippery surface is unavoidable, brake before you reach it and pedal slowly through. Most importantly, ride within your limits and don't take corners faster than you know you can do safely.

When descending hills, stay completely aware of what's going on around you. Listen for vehicles approaching from behind while keeping an eye on the road ahead; watch for pedestrians, dogs, or cars that may cross your path and look for conditions that will have to be avoided. When descending a steep trail, shift your weight behind the seat to avoid pitching yourself over the handlebars. Keep both hands on the brakes and stay loose and light on the bike, letting your arms and legs absorb the bumps on the trail. Perhaps most importantly, visualize the line you will take and stick to it as much as possible. Your bike goes where you look, so if you desperately try to avoid an obstacle, you will likely ride into it.

Various trail conditions may require adjusting your riding technique. When going through mud, maintain constant motion to avoid getting stuck. Aim your bike right through a puddle—mud is firmest in the middle—and don't stop pedaling. When out of the water, pulse your brakes to dry the rims. In soft sand, keep your weight evenly balanced and pedal steadily in a low gear without making any drastic turns.

Equipment and Clothing

- Use protective eyewear—sunglasses or glasses with clear lenses will keep water, dirt, bugs, and rain out of your eyes.
- Carry a Camelbak or at least one water bottle. For hot-weather rides, fill your water bottle halfway and put in the freezer the night before. The morning of your ride, fill it to the top. You'll have ice-cold water for at least part of your ride.
- Cycling gloves will protect your hands and help maintain the circulation in your fingers.
- Cycling shorts and jerseys are made of materials that wick moisture

away from the skin, unlike cotton, which retains dampness. A jersey with pockets—or perhaps a saddlebag or handlebar bag—is also practical for keeping snacks and other necessities out of the way but within easy reach.

- Carry a spare tube, patch kit, air pump, and tire levers. If you puncture a tire and don't have the tools to fix it, it's okay to ride on the flat slowly for a few miles without damaging the rim. If you're flatting often, you may not be inflating your tires enough.
- Have a healthy respect for the sun. Use sunscreen year-round, even on cloudy days. Clothing is the best protection, so if the weather permits, wear a tightly woven long-sleeve shirt or jersey. Wear a helmet with a visor and wraparound sunglasses with ultraviolet-blocking lenses.
- Carry bug repellent, especially when riding off-road.
- Ride on a saddle that's comfortable and positioned at the right height.
- Cold-weather riding requires some additional gear; fatigue combined with damp clothing and a biting wind chill can quickly lead to hypothermia. Dress in layers: synthetic fabrics underneath to wick moisture away from your skin, an insulating garment, and a breathable layer on top. Wind-resistant tights are essential and come in varying degrees of thickness. Wear thin, over-the-ankle sock liners; neoprene booties or toe covers on your shoes; and Gore-Tex gloves on your hands. Since you can lose up to 40 percent of your body heat from your head and neck, it's smart to wear a synthetic cap under your helmet.

Food and Drink

Pro racers understand the critical link between nutrition and performance, and even the occasional cyclist can take lessons from them. You're fueled by food, and what you choose to eat during a ride will affect your performance and how you feel. A ride on a hot day can bring misery if you're dehydrated, overheated, or hungry.

Energy bars and gels provide instant energy and are easy to carry. Fig bars, cereal bars, and dried apricots are also good sources of carbohydrates with little fat. Plus, they're small and won't get squished in a saddle bag or jersey pocket.

Drink often during exercise—before you feel thirsty—to stay hydrated. On a long hot ride you can sweat more than 3 quarts of water an hour. Restore fluids and electrolytes after a ride with sports drinks or water.

Commercial sports drinks are a good source of fluids, electrolytes, and carbohydrates, which will help you stay hydrated and sustain energy. Beverages that contain caffeine or alcohol increase dehydration, so avoid them during a ride.

Lyme Disease

Lyme disease is a tick-borne multisystem inflammatory illness named for the Connecticut town where the first case was reported. The bacteria that causes Lyme disease is transmitted from the bite of a deer tick. In 1998 there were more than 3,400 reported cases of Lyme disease in Connecticut; New England is considered a high-risk area. It generally takes from 24 to 36 hours for infection to set in, so prompt removal of ticks is vitally important. A common sign of infection is a skin rash in the bite area; other symptoms of Lyme disease are vaguely flulike: joint pain, fever, lethargy, and loss of appetite. Left untreated, the infection can progress to more serious stages, affecting the heart, muscles and joints, and the central nervous system. Antibiotics are effective in treating the infection, especially if diagnosed early. A vaccine has also been developed to prevent Lyme disease.

When riding off-road, especially in tall grass and in brushy or wooded areas, take protective measures. Wear light-colored clothing and use an insect repellent made specifically for ticks. Avoid riding off trails or sitting on the ground in grassy or wooded areas. After every ride—especially in the spring and summer months when ticks are most prevalent—brush off clothing outside, then check your skin carefully (nymph-stage deer ticks are tiny, about the size of a poppy seed) and remove any ticks. It's a good idea to have someone else check your head, parting your hair and looking at the scalp. If you are bitten, save the tick for later testing in case a problem develops, and check the bite area for about a month for the appearance of a skin rash. For more information, call the state's Lyme Disease Foundation at 860-525-2000.

Further Reading and Resources

Publications

Bicycling magazine
Box 7308
Red Oak, IA 51591-0308
1-800-666-2806
web site: www.bicyclingmagazine.com

The Ride magazine
678 Cortland Circle, Suite 16
Cheshire, CT 06410
e-mail: RideZine@aol.com
Publishes weekly club ride and race schedules and is sold in most bike shops.

Connecticut/Rhode Island Atlas & Gazetteer
DeLorme Publishing Company
P.O. Box 298
Yarmouth, ME 04096
207-846-7000
Provides topographical maps of Connecticut in 42 detailed sections. This is an invaluable supplement to the maps in this book. The atlas can be found in most bookstores around the state.

The Connecticut Bicycle Book
The Connecticut Bicycle Coalition
One Union Place
Hartford, CT 06103
A comprehensive directory covering numerous topics including racing, touring, bike laws, and advocacy.

Bicycling Organizations and Advocacy Groups
No matter what kind of cycling you do—commuting, racing, long-distance road touring, or recreation—cycling advocacy affects you. It's every cyclist's responsibility to become educated and ride safely.

New England Mountain Bike Association (NEMBA)
P.O. Box 2221

Acton, MA 01720
1-800-57-NEMBA
web site: www.nemba.org

Connecticut NEMBA
P.O. Box 290956
Wethersfield, CT 06129-9956
860-676-9721
web site: www.members.home.net/bnemba
A nonprofit organization dedicated to promoting trail access and educating mountain bikers on being responsible trail users.

Connecticut Bike Coalition (CBC)
One Union Place
Hartford, CT 06103
860-527-5200
e-mail: CTBIKECOAL@aol.com
An organization of cycling clubs, bike shops, and individuals dedicated to promoting bicycle transportation, recreation, and safety through advocacy, public education, and cycling events.

International Mountain Biking Association (IMBA)
P.O. Box 7578
Boulder, CO 80306
303-545-9011
web site: www.imba.com
e-mail: imba@aol.com
A nonprofit advocacy organization promoting environmentally sound and socially responsible mountain biking.

Bicycle Federation of America
1506 21st Street, NW
Suite 200
Washington, DC 20036
202-463-6622
web site: www.bikefed.org
A national bike organization that helps state and local cycling-advocacy groups in obtaining federal funds for bike projects and helps the Department of Transportation and other federal agencies to develop bike-friendly policies and guidelines.

THE
LITCHFIELD
HILLS

1. The Covered Bridge to Lime Rock

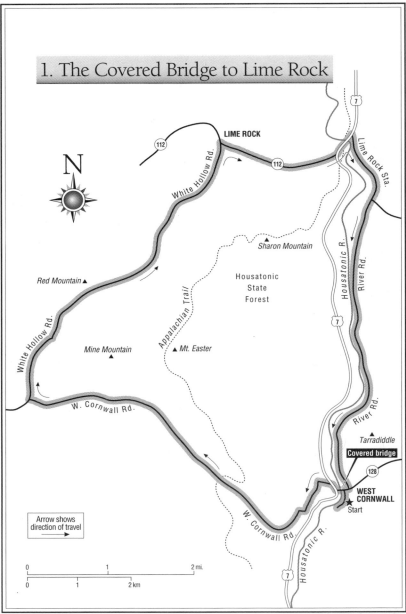

N

LIME ROCK

112

112

White Hollow Rd.

Lime Rock Sta.

Sharon Mountain

Red Mountain ▲

Housatonic
State
Forest

Housatonic R.

River Rd.

Appalachian Trail

White Hollow Rd.

Mine Mountain ▲

▲ Mt. Easter

W. Cornwall Rd.

River Rd.

▲ Tarradiddle

Covered bridge

128

WEST
CORNWALL
★ Start

W. Cornwall Rd.

Housatonic R.

Arrow shows
direction of travel
→

0   1   2 mi.
0   1   2 km

Paul Woodward, © 2000 The Countryman Press

1

The Covered Bridge to Lime Rock

Distance: 16.2 miles
Terrain: *Rolling hills with a couple of short, steep climbs; one 2.5-mile dirt road along the Housatonic River (with an alternate paved route)*
Difficulty: *Moderate*
Recommended bicycle: *Touring/road bike*

The high elevations of Connecticut's northwest corner will challenge cyclists, but those who take on the rugged hills are rewarded with spectacular vistas of forested ridgelines, deep ravines, and cool forests of hemlock, pine, and maple. This area is equally prized for its quiet roads and pastoral surroundings.

This tour is a pleasant introduction to this rural corner of the state. You will begin at the much-photographed landmark red covered bridge that spans the Housatonic River between Sharon and the village of West Cornwall, an attractive cluster of homes that spreads along the river and up into the high hills. As you pedal over the wooden floorboards of the one-lane bridge—noted bridge architect Ithiel Town designed it in 1837—you'll hear one of the river's prime stretches of white water churning below. Kayakers and canoeists flock to the covered bridge during the spring thaw, when the thundering rapids are at their best. It was Oliver Wendell Holmes who said, "There's no tonic like the Housatonic," a sentiment shared by those fortunate enough to live near its banks and by the many who play in and around it.

Meandering roads will bring you to centuries-old homesteads high above the river in Sharon before you coast down and follow its downstream course back to the covered bridge. This area puts on an impressive natural show in autumn, when foliage burns brightly in the hills rising precipitously from the riverbank.

The closest spot for food and other supplies is Baird's General Store, a few miles south on US 7 in Cornwall Bridge. West Cornwall has a couple of eateries—Café by the Bridge, a stone's throw from the covered bridge at the corner of Lower River Road, is a friendly, casual spot for breakfast and lunch. Café Lally, on Railroad Street, offers vegetarian cuisine.

Be sure to save time to explore West Cornwall. Don't miss Ian Ingersoll's studio and showroom in the white tollhouse near the covered bridge. His beautifully handcrafted, Shaker-style furniture reflects the Shaker ideals of simplicity and practicality. Also in the village is the Cornwall Bridge Pottery Store, where you can see the designs of award-winning potter Todd Piker as well as the work of other local artisans. Piker's studio, including a 40-foot-long wood-burning kiln, is downstream in Cornwall Bridge, at the foot of Bald Mountain.

Directions for the Ride

The ride starts at the covered bridge in West Cornwall, on the Housatonic River at the junction of US 7 and CT 128. From US 7, cross the bridge and take an immediate right; park here along Lower River Road.

0.0 *From Lower River Road, cross the covered bridge and bear right toward US 7 North. At the stop sign, turn right on US 7, then take an immediate left onto West Cornwall Road.*

The road ascends past fields and stone walls before winding into the rocky hills and thick forest above the river. Two steep climbs start the ride, followed by a long, gently rolling section. If you look carefully to the left during the ascent, you'll catch dramatic views of the hills plunging toward the Housatonic River.

Although this backcountry road is the most direct route connecting the villages of West Cornwall and Sharon, it remains very quiet and little used. The Appalachian Trail, marked by white blazes, cuts across West Cornwall Road on its route from Georgia to Maine—51 miles across Connecticut. The Roy Swamp Wildlife Management Area and the Miles Wildlife Sanctuary protect a large tract of wetland for a variety of birds and other wildlife.

5.1 *Bear right onto White Hollow Road.*

A 19th-century bridge over the Housatonic River.

Here the flat section along marshes and swamps changes to a gradual descent past fields and farms. You can glimpse views of Housatonic State Forest, including 1,275-foot Mine Mountain, as you cruise downhill into Salisbury.

9.5 *Turn right at the stop sign (just past the Lime Rock Park infield entrance) onto Lime Rock Road (CT 112) in the village of Lime Rock.*

The Lime Rock section of Salisbury is a quaint village presided over by one of the country's premier racetracks. Lime Rock Park (860-435-0896) hosts vintage automobile races, professional and amateur road racing, and car festivals. It is also home to the Skip Barber Racing and Driving Schools.

10.9 *Bear left where CT 112 forks just past White Hollow Farm. (To avoid the final stretch of this tour, which travels along a dirt road, turn right and follow US 7 south to the covered bridge in West Cornwall.)*

11.0 *Turn left onto US 7. At the traffic light (at the Canaan town line) turn right onto Lime Rock Station.*

Use caution on the road ahead; you will pass over several railroad crossings.

12.2 Bear right at the junction of Lime Rock Station and Music Mountain Road.

Music Mountain (860-364-2080), in the tiny community of Falls Village, is America's oldest continuous summer chamber music festival, entertaining music lovers from its 120-acre mountaintop location since 1930. Jazz, folk, classical, and chamber music concerts are performed by international artists from mid-June to early September.

12.6 Continue straight as Lime Rock Station turns into River Road, a hard-packed dirt road winding between railroad tracks and the Housatonic River.

This secluded area is protected by the Weantinoge Heritage Land Trust. Many prime picnic spots can be found as you follow the river downstream on its slow course toward West Cornwall. You may pass an occasional fly-fisherman, but little else in the way of civilization. In about 2.5 miles, River Road will return to pavement.

16.1 Turn right at the stop sign onto Sharon-Goshen Turnpike (CT 128) into the center of West Cornwall.

Just before reaching the covered bridge, turn left onto Lower River Road to bring you back to where the ride began.

Bicycle Shops

The Bike Doctor & Sports Center, 97 Church Street (US 44), Canaan; 860-824-5577

Cycle Loft, 25 Commons Drive (US 202), Litchfield; 860-567-1713

2
New Preston to Bulls Bridge

Distance: *30 miles*
Terrain: *Rolling with a couple of long, sustained climbs; a 1-mile dirt road*
Difficulty: *Strenuous*
Recommended bicycle: *Touring/road bike*

The tiny roadside village of New Preston was nothing more than a cluster of worn 19th-century mill buildings a couple of decades ago. Since then it has been spruced up and resurrected into a charming enclave of antiques shops and art galleries that attracts droves of weekend visitors. You'll follow the east branch of the Aspetuck River out of the village to the shore of Lake Waramaug, one of the state's most unspoiled and beautiful lakes, which draws comparisons to Switzerland's Lake Lucerne.

Leaving the lakeshore, country roads wind through an old-fashioned landscape of farmland and scattered Colonial homesteads as they meander toward the Housatonic River.

Bulls Bridge is one of Connecticut's two remaining covered bridges still open to vehicular traffic (the other is a few miles upstream in West Cornwall). The first bridge at this site near the New York border was built in 1760 by Isaac Bull; later, Jacob Bull built a covered bridge here in 1811. The bridge itself, or the narrow trail leading upstream from it, are good vantage points for watching paddlers maneuver the gorge's churning white-water and boulder-strewn rapids. The weather-beaten brown bridge, rebuilt in 1842, attracts many artists who set up their easels near the Housatonic River.

The upscale roadside village of Kent is a vibrant arts community, especially in fall when leaf peepers descend on the hills. Main Street is

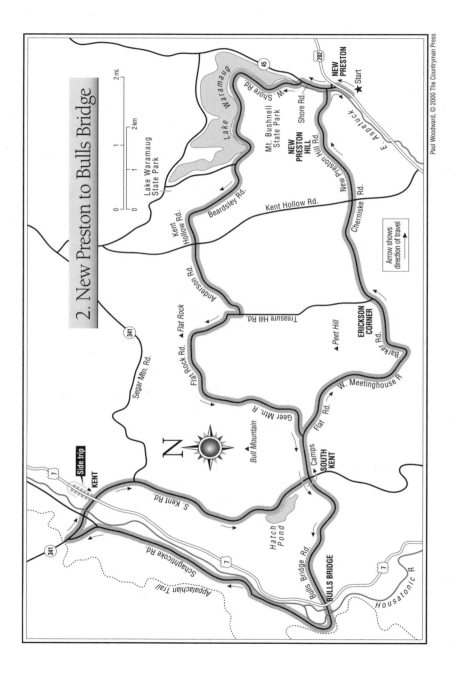

2. New Preston to Bulls Bridge

Lake Waramaug State Park

Lake Waramaug

Mt. Bushnell State Park

NEW PRESTON HILL

NEW PRESTON

Start

W. Shore Rd.

Shore Rd.

Kent Hollow Rd.

Beardsley Rd.

Kent Hollow Rd.

New Preston Hill Rd.

E. Aspetuck

Cherniske Rd.

Anderson Rd.

▲ Flat Rock

Flat Rock Rd.

Treasure Hill Rd.

Peet Hill ▲

ERICKSON CORNER

Barkley Rd.

Arrow shows direction of travel →

Segar Mtn. Rd.

N

Geer Mtn. R.

Bull Mountain ▲

W. Meetinghouse R.

Flat Rd.

Camps

SOUTH KENT

Side trip

KENT

S. Kent Rd.

Schaghticoke Rd.

Appalachian Trail

Hatch Pond

Bulls Bridge Rd.

BULLS BRIDGE

Housatonic R.

Paul Woodward, © 2000 The Countryman Press

packed with cafés, boutiques, galleries, and antiques shops, making it perfect for strolling.

Directions for the Ride

Park in the New Preston section of Washington, either at the dirt parking area on New Milford Turnpike (US 202) just west of the intersection of East Shore Road (CT 45), or on East Shore Road in front of the small park and waterfall in the village.

0.0 Head up East Shore Road into New Preston.

As you pass through the village, the yellow clapboard community hall and a row of tiny shops will be on the left.

0.5 At the stop sign, turn left onto West Shore Road.

This will take you on a narrow, twisting road that hugs the edge of Lake Waramaug.

3.4 Turn left onto Golf Links Road.

Climb and descend a short, steep hill past the Lake Waramaug Country Club and its golf course.

3.7 Turn right onto Beardsley Road.

Cruise downhill past a smattering of antique homes and farms, including Constitution Oak Farm, a rambling 1840 farmhouse, now a bed & breakfast. An oak tree on the property is said to be a descendant of Connecticut's famous Constitution Oak.

4.6 Turn left onto Kent Hollow Road.

Go straight across the four-way intersection onto Anderson Road. Here you'll begin a strenuous 1.5-mile climb through the woods past a few country estates.

6.5 At the stop sign, turn right onto Treasure Hill Road.

This area of thick forest on Ore Hill is protected by the Iron Mountain Preserve and the Nature Conservancy. The unspoiled 300-acre tract has a 1.5-mile-loop hiking trail; the trailhead will be on the left as you travel down Treasure Hill Road.

7.3 Turn left onto Richards Road.

7.6 At the yield sign, bear left onto Flat Rock Road.

A horse farm on New Preston Hill.

This quiet road hugs a ridgeline with spectacular views of the Litchfield Hills to the west.

8.4 Turn left onto Geer Mountain Road.

Use caution on this very steep descent past Iron Mountain Farm.

10.2 At the stop sign, turn right onto Camps Flat Road.

10.8 *At the next stop sign, go straight across South Kent Road onto Bulls Bridge Road.*

You will pass the rural South Kent School, a private school for boys founded in 1923 by two graduates of the Kent School, a campus you'll ride by later.

13.2 *At the traffic light, go straight across Kent Road (US 7).*

On the corner, at 248 Bulls Bridge Road, is the historic Judd House, home of the American Heritage Shop. This handsome 1830 clapboard house sells beautifully crafted American country furniture and accessories.

If you turn left on US 7, just past Bulls Bridge Inn is the Country Mart, a small general store with ready-made sandwiches, snacks, and drinks.

13.3 *Cross Bulls Bridge.*

George Washington made a note in his diaries of a mishap crossing the bridge in March 1781 while traveling from New York en route to meetings with the French in Newport. The bridge was undergoing repairs, and although historians debate the details, a horse fell into the water. Washington penned in his expense ledger: "Getting a horse out of Bulls Falls, $215." This was a considerable sum in the 18th century, which leads one to believe that the steed belonged to the commander-in-chief.

Later, the area's rich sources of iron ore were transported across the bridge to forges and blast furnaces in Kent during much of the 19th century. During the Revolution, the covered bridge was a vital link between the supply depot in Lebanon and Washington's headquarters in New York, on the road known as the "galloping highway."

13.6 *Pass under a wooden truss, then take the first right onto Schaghticoke Road.*

This solitary road follows the Housatonic River into the village of Kent, passing by the tiny Schaghticoke Indian Reservation, which consists of a burying ground and a few buildings. The Appalachian Trail runs above the road on the left. About 1 mile of this 4.3-mile road is hard-packed dirt, but it's easily passable on a road bike.

17.9 *At the stop sign, turn right onto Bridge Street (CT 341).*

On the banks of the Housatonic River is the campus of the Kent School, started in 1906 by an Episcopal monk. The Reverend Hotchkiss Still opened the private school for boys in a farmhouse. Today, the coed campus is housed in handsome Georgian brick buildings.

18.6 *At the traffic light at the southern edge of Kent, continue straight onto Maple Street (CT 341).*

Side Trip: Turning left onto Main Street, you'll pass many art galleries and boutiques, a well-stocked bookstore, and a handful of delis and bakeries. Don't miss Stosh's Ice Cream in the restored Kent Railroad Station, a local landmark that is exceedingly popular among tourists and locals. Stosh's makes all its ice cream, sorbet, and frozen yogurt using local dairy-farm cream. For baked goods and sandwiches, another Main Street landmark is the Stroble Baking Company. For coffee, try the Kent Coffee & Chocolate Company.

19.3 *Go straight onto South Kent Road (CT 341 goes left here). This easy, flat stretch of road follows the shore of Hatch Pond.*

22.3 *Turn left onto Camp Flats Road.*

25.0 *At the stop sign, go straight onto Barker Road.*

At about a mile, Barker Road turns into Cherniske Road.

28.0 *At the stop sign, continue straight onto New Preston Hill Road.*

This is the last climb of the day, a 1-mile ascent of New Preston Hill. At its crest, you'll pass the Stone Church on a tiny green overlooking pastel-colored barns and gently sloping pastures. From here, a quick descent will bring you back into New Preston.

30.0 *At the stop sign, turn right into the center of New Preston and end the tour.*

Bicycle Shops

Bike Express, 73 Bridge Street (CT 67 and US 202), New Milford; 860-354-1466

Cycle Loft, 25 Commons Drive (US 202), Litchfield; 860-567-1713

3
Lake Waramaug

Distance: *8.7 miles*
Terrain: *An easy, mostly level loop*
Difficulty: *Easy*
Recommended bicycle: *Touring/road bike*

This scenic 8-mile ride around the intricate shoreline of Lake Wara-maug begins in the 19th-century mill town of New Preston. Today it's a tony enclave of antiques shops along the East Aspetuck River, but at one time there were more than two dozen factories and mills here pro-ducing everything from hats and sleighs to horseshoes and bricks. The Civil War era brought an end to this; however, some of the carefully preserved mill buildings remain.

The route around this lake—named for a Native American sachem—is virtually flat, a rarity in the state's rugged western highlands. If the ride doesn't feel complete without a lung-searing climb, try conquering Tan-ner Hill Road, off Lake Road (CT 45), just north of Boulders Inn. If you make it to the top, you'll be duly rewarded with a breathtaking panorama of the lake and its green-clad hills; you may realize why so many visitors remark on its similarity to the alpine lakes of Austria and Switzerland.

Hopkins Vineyard sits in the hills above the lake's north shore. The family-owned winery is considered one of the most scenic in the North-east. The Hopkins Farm was started here in 1787 when Elijah Hopkins returned from the War of Independence and began farming the hills. Since then, the farm has diversified, raising race horses, sheep, and dairy cows and growing tobacco. The first grapevines were planted in 1979.

This 3-mile-long lake has been drawing visitors since the mid-1800s, evidenced by the rambling shingle cottages and turn-of-the-century inns strung along its banks. The inns and restaurants are lovely but pricey;

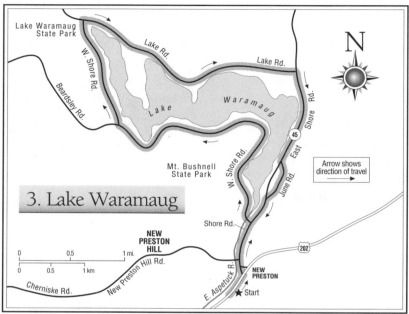

Paul Woodward, © 2000 The Countryman Press

Lake Waramaug State Park offers more rustic lodgings, with 88 wooded and open campsites along the lake's west shore. Each spring the lake hosts the Eastern Women's Intercollegiate Crew Races, which draws rowers from dozens of universities and colleges along the East Coast to compete for the Governor's Cup.

For food and supplies, go to the Warren's General Store several miles north on CT 45, or head east on US 202 and CT 47 into Washington Depot, or west on US 202 to a convenience store in Marbledale.

Directions for the Ride

Start in the dirt parking lot on New Milford Turnpike (US 202) just west of its junction with East Shore Road (CT 45) in the New Preston section of Washington. There are also a few parking spots in the village on East Shore Road, in front of the waterfall.

0.0 With your back to US 202, follow East Shore Road (CT 45)

Lake Waramaug as seen from Tanner Hill.

through the tiny roadside village of New Preston.

The village sits near Lake Waramaug's southeast tip. A quaint northern Italian café and an old-fashioned pharmacy sit among the trove of antiques shops. As you leave the village, East Shore Road climbs gently toward the lake and passes a stunning, recently restored red mill on the Aspetuck River.

0.5 Facing the Washington town beach parking lot at the intersection of West Shore Road and East Shore Road (CT 45), turn left onto West Shore Road.

This scenic stretch twists along the lakeshore and offers dramatic views at every turn. It is often busy on weekends with motorists, cyclists, and walkers, so use caution, especially on the sharp corners.

3.4 Continue following the shore road to the right (Golf Links Road is straight ahead).

3.9 Pass through Lake Waramaug State Park, then continue following the lakeshore into Warren, as the road changes to North Shore Road.

The picnic tables along the shore of this 95-acre park are an ideal place to rest or lunch. In autumn, it's also a good spot to see the bright hues of foliage reflected on the lake's surface.

Side Trip: An interesting side trip here is to Hopkins Vineyard, which sits at the crest of a short hill off the lakeshore. The winery is housed in a 19th-century barn selling wine, gourmet food items, and gifts; the hayloft wine bar has a beautiful view of the lake.

Next door to the vineyard is the Hopkins Inn, which began taking in summer visitors from New York in 1847. The yellow clapboard inn sits atop a hill with a spectacular view of the lake from the stone terrace of its restaurant, whose Austrian cuisine has a rave following.

6.6 *At the stop sign, turn right onto East Shore Road (CT 45).*

8.2 *Continue straight through the four-way intersection on East Shore Road (CT 45). Retracing your route through New Preston will bring you to the end of the ride.*

Bicycle Shops

Bike Express, 73 Bridge Street (CT 67 and US 202), New Milford; 860-354-1466

Cycle Loft, 25 Commons Drive (US 202), Litchfield; 860-567-1713

4

Washington Depot to Bethlehem

Distance: *23.8 miles*
Terrain: *Low hills with a few steep climbs*
Difficulty: *Moderate to strenuous*
Recommended bicycle: *Touring/road bike*

This ride features the colonial villages of Washington and Bethlehem, linked by back roads through rolling farm country.

A winding climb up Green Hill will bring you to the lovely hilltop village of Washington, with its vintage Colonial clapboard homes, white-spired First Congregational Church, and neat picket fences standing sentinel over the green. During the Revolution, Washington was a hotbed for loyal followers of the fiery patriot Ethan Allen. In fact, this former community of Old Judea became the first in the country to change its name in honor of the nation's first president and the first town in Connecticut to become incorporated after the Declaration of Independence was signed. Washington passed through town three times on his way toward the Hudson, stopping for a meal in 1774 at the Cogswell Tavern in the New Preston section of town.

In the early part of the 20th century there were about 60 dairy farms in town; today it's a haven for urbanites, with only a few working farms remaining. Washington Depot, at the base of Green Hill, is the business center of town. The Washington Market has a good deli; picnic supplies can be found at the Pantry on Titus Road and at Jack's Market on Bee Brook Road (CT 47). The Hickory Stick Bookshop is a beautiful store with an impressive array of titles; many bestselling authors sign their work here.

Bethlehem was still wilderness in 1740, when settlers brought the Reverend Joseph Bellamy to their outpost. It was Bellamy who named the

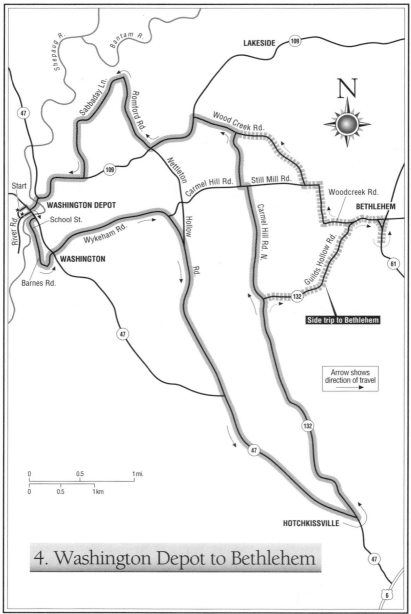

Shepaug R.

Bantam R.

LAKESIDE 109

Sabbaday Ln.

Romford Rd.

N

47

Wood Creek Rd.

109

Nettleton

Carmel Hill Rd.

Still Mill Rd.

Woodcreek Rd.

Start

BETHLEHEM

WASHINGTON DEPOT

School St.

River Rd.

Hollow Rd.

Carmel Hill Rd. N.

Guilds Hollow Rd.

61

Wykeham Rd.

WASHINGTON

Barnes Rd.

132

Side trip to Bethlehem

47

Arrow shows
direction of travel

132

47

| 0 | 0.5 | 1 mi. |
| 0 | 0.5 | 1 km |

HOTCHKISSVILLE

4. Washington Depot to Bethlehem

47

6

Paul Woodward, © 2000 The Countryman Press

town after the birthplace of Jesus; he also founded the nation's first theological seminary and became known as "The Pope of Litchfield County." The 1754 Bellamy-Ferriday House (203-266-7596) on the green was once his modest cottage; over generations it was transformed into a stately 13-room Palladian mansion. The estate and its spectacular formal gardens of lilacs, peonies, and roses can be toured from mid-May through October, 11–4 Wednesday and weekends. It's listed on the National Register of Historic Places and is surrounded by 80 acres of woods protected by the Bethlehem Land Trust.

Bethlehem is lovingly known as "the Christmas Town" by the hordes of people who drive from miles away to stamp their Christmas cards at the village post office. For more than 60 years, local artists have been designing ink stamps and seals for customers to decorate their envelopes with.

Thousands of people descend on this quiet New England town in September for Litchfield County's second-largest fair. The annual Christmas Town Festival draws nearly as many in December.

Directions for the Ride

Park in Washington Depot, either along River Road near the junction of Green Hill Road (CT 47) or in Bryan Memorial Plaza across from the town hall. Washington Depot can be reached from CT 109, CT 47, or US 202.

0.0 From the stop sign on River Road, turn right onto Green Hill Road (CT 47), immediately crossing the Shepaug River.

0.1 After the bridge, take the first right onto School Street, which crosses in front of Washington Primary School.

School Street turns into Barnes Road and climbs gradually to the Washington green.

1.0 Barnes Road turns right; proceed straight onto Rossiter Road.

Noted architect Ehrick Rossiter designed many of the elegant homes around the Washington green.

1.1 At the stop sign, turn left onto Kirby Road.

This will bring you to the Washington green and the Gunnery, an

The First Congregational Church on the Washington green.

exclusive private school founded by village resident and abolitionist Frederick Gunn. The school, which opened in 1850 in a schoolhouse, now occupies many buildings on the green, including a Tudor estate. The attractive Washington Green General Store shares a white clapboard building with the village post office.

1.3 *At the second stop sign, turn right onto Green Hill Road (CT 47).*

1.4 *Immediately turn left onto Wykeham Road.*

Follow Wykeham Road past the Gunn Historical Museum, a 1781 house museum, and Gunn Memorial Library, built in 1908.

2.6 *At the intersection of Old Litchfield Road, continue straight on Wykeham Road.*

You'll pass many fine examples of well-preserved Colonial architecture along this rolling country road.

3.4 *Bear right onto Tompkins Hill Road.*

Use caution on this very steep descent.

3.9 *At the stop sign, turn right onto Nettleton Hollow Road.*

This road gently descends toward Woodbury.

6.8 *At the stop sign, turn left onto Washington Road (CT 47).*

9.9 *Turn left onto Weekeepeemee Road (CT 132) into the village of Hotchkissville.*

Stay on CT 132 as it turns into Carmel Hill Road South (Weekeepeemee Road will continue to the right) and crosses the Bethlehem town line. Begin a slow, 4-mile climb past hilltop farms on Carmel Hill.

14.0 *At the crest of the hill, turn left (CT 132 continues to the right) and proceed a short distance to a stop sign. Bear left onto Carmel Hill Road North.*

Side Trip: To visit the Bethlehem green, continue on CT 132 and descend a long hill that will bring you to the town center. Rejoin the ride by retracing your way on CT 132 for a short time and turning right onto Wood Creek Road, which connects with the main loop in Washington.

16.2 *Stay on Carmel Hill Road as it bends to the left at the intersection of Still Hill Road, then remain on Carmel Hill Road as it makes a right turn at the intersection of Woods Edge Road.*

Use caution as you descend steep Carmel Hill Road.

17.1 *At the stop sign, turn left onto Wood Creek Road.*

This quiet, twisting road will return you to Washington.

17.9 *At the stop sign, turn left onto Litchfield Road (CT 109).*

18.9 *Turn right onto Romford Road.*

20.3 *Turn left onto Sabbaday Lane.*

This sprawling horse farm sits on the edge of the Steep Rock Reservation Land Trust.

22.5 *At the stop sign, turn right onto Blackville Road (CT 109).*

23.5 *Turn left at the next stop sign onto Bee Brook Road (CT 47/CT 109).*

23.7 *In Washington Depot, turn left onto Green Hill Road (CT 47).*

23.8 *Take the first right onto River Road, where the ride ends.*

Bicycle Shops

Bike Express, 73 Bridge Street (CT 67 and US 202), New Milford; 860-354-1466

Cycle Loft, 25 Commons Drive (US 202), Litchfield; 860-567-1713

5

Steep Rock Reservation

Distance: 14 miles
Terrain: *Rolling dirt roads with two steep climbs and some level riding;
two paved sections*
Difficulty: Moderate
Recommended bicycle: *Mountain bike*

This secluded reservation sits on nearly 2,000 rugged acres in Washington and New Milford, sliced in two by the boulder-strewn Shepaug River, which the Native Americans named for its rocky waters. A 26-mile section of the river has been designated wild, largely through the preservation efforts of the Steep Rock Association. The river leaves Steep Rock and flows through the peaceful backwater community of Judds Bridge on the edge of the reservation before joining Lake Lillinonah several miles to the south. It was Princess Lillinonah's father, Chief Waramaug, who sold land in Washington to the early colonists.

The hiking trails that snake up the hills and along the ridgelines are closed to mountain bikes because of the fragile condition of some due to erosion and overuse. Cyclists are allowed only on the trail and dirt road that are part of this route. Most of this ride follows the little-used dirt roads in New Milford and Roxbury that circle the reservation.

You can also ride on a portion of abandoned railroad bed that parallels the Shepaug River. In the early part of the 20th century, the Shepaug, Litchfield, and Northern rail line connected Litchfield to railroad lines in southern Connecticut, hauling produce to New York City and summer visitors to the Litchfield Hills. Trains rumbled along the serpentine river on 32 miles of track with 193 curves and a 495-foot tunnel. The last train passed through in 1948.

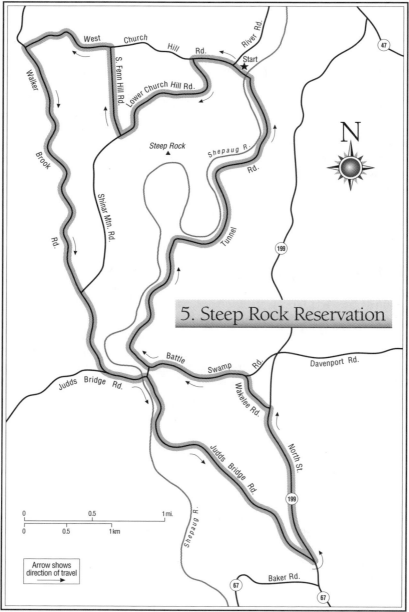

West Church Hill Rd. River Rd.

Start

47

S. Fenn Hill Rd.

Lower Church Hill Rd.

Walker

Brook

Steep Rock

Shepaug R. Rd.

Shinar Mtn. Rd.

Rd.

Tunnel

199

5. Steep Rock Reservation

Battle Swamp Rd.

Davenport Rd.

Judds Bridge Rd.

Wakelee Rd.

Judds Bridge Rd.

North St.

N

199

0   0.5   1 mi.
0   0.5   1km

Shepaug R.

Arrow shows
direction of travel

Baker Rd.

67

67

Paul Woodward, © 2000 The Countryman Press

Directions for the Ride

The ride begins at the entrance to the Steep Rock Reservation on River Road in Washington Depot. From CT 47 in the center of the Depot, turn onto River Road and follow it along the Shepaug River for about 1.5 miles. Turn left into the unmarked dirt parking area, at the signpost for Lower Church Hill Road and Tunnel Road.

0.0 *Go to the paved road (Lower Church Hill Road) and head uphill.*

This is a strenuous climb—the ride's toughest—that winds through the woods, circling around the edge of the land trust.

0.3 *Bear left to continue on Lower Church Hill Road (West Church Hill Road, a dirt road, goes to the right).*

The road soon flattens and follows stone walls and huge oaks as you pass some of the meadows and rural 18th-century estates that look out on the upper edge of the reservation.

1.4 *Turn right onto Fenn Hill Road.*

A moderate climb here takes you along broad fields of tall grass. This is a good spot for viewing deer, fox, turkey, and other wildlife, especially early in the day or at dusk.

2.3 *At the T-intersection, turn left onto West Church Hill Road.*

A fun, winding descent brings you through farmland before plunging into the woods. The road narrows and turns to dirt near the bottom, so use caution.

3.0 *At the stop sign, turn left onto Walker Brook Road South (unmarked).*

This secluded dirt road follows the banks of Walker Brook on flat, easy terrain. A few cottages and farms are on this road, but it is unlikely that you will encounter cars or people in this beautiful area on the Washington/New Milford town line.

3.6 *After crossing a small wooden bridge, continue straight (an unmarked dirt road heads left).*

5.0 *At the intersection of Shinar Mountain Road (to the left), continue straight.*

5.7 *Here you enter the old farming community of Judds Bridge. At the T-intersection, bear left onto Judds Bridge Road (unmarked).*

This peaceful enclave is nothing more than a cluster of centuries-old homesteads and farms on the banks of the Shepaug River, connected by dirt roads and a wooden bridge. Time has dramatically stood still in this hidden valley in Roxbury.

6.0 *Cross the wooden bridge and turn right to continue on Judds Bridge Road.*

Follow the Shepaug River upstream. After about 0.5 mile, look into the woods on the left for a boulder inscribed with a memorial to Allen S. Hurlburt, a first selectman in Roxbury for 29 years.

7.5 *At the four-way intersection, continue straight.*

8.2 *At the stop sign, turn left onto North Street (CT 199).*

This is the last paved section of the tour.

9.5 *Turn left onto Wakelee Road.*

Descend this quiet back road until you see a large white Colonial home on your left; turn left onto the narrow road just past it (Battle Swamp Road). You will pass a few barns before the road turns to dirt, climbs a steep hill, then sharply descends the other side. The surface is sometimes loose and potholed; use caution and begin braking well in advance of the stop sign.

10.6 *At the stop sign, turn right onto Tunnel Road.*

You are now back at Judds Bridge, but only for a short time. When the road rises into the woods, look for a row of boulders marking a trailhead on the left.

11.0 *At this trailhead, ride around the boulders and onto a wide dirt trail, which will take you into the Steep Rock Reservation.*

This trail starts as hard-packed dirt but becomes rocky as you pass under the power lines. When you reenter the woods, the trail becomes rough and very poorly drained, especially in spring. At the top, pass through another row of boulders.

11.8 *At the Y-intersection, bear right.*

You will see green signs designating the back entrance to the Steep

A rural dirt road in Judds Bridge.

Rock Reservation. From this spot above the railroad tunnel, descend a loose rocky section of Tunnel Road, which will flatten out and follow the Shepaug River upstream for about 2 miles. This area is popular with hikers, mountain bikers, equestrians, and occasional motorists. When approaching horses, dismount and wait until they pass. If approaching from behind, make riders aware of your presence.

13.6 *At the three-way intersection, bear left to continue following the river.*

13.9 *At the riding ring, bear left and cross the bridge to return to the parking lot and end the ride.*

Bicycle Shops

Bike Express, 73 Bridge Street (CT 67 and US 202), New Milford; 860-354-1466

Cycle Loft, 25 Commons Drive (US 202), Litchfield; 860-567-1713

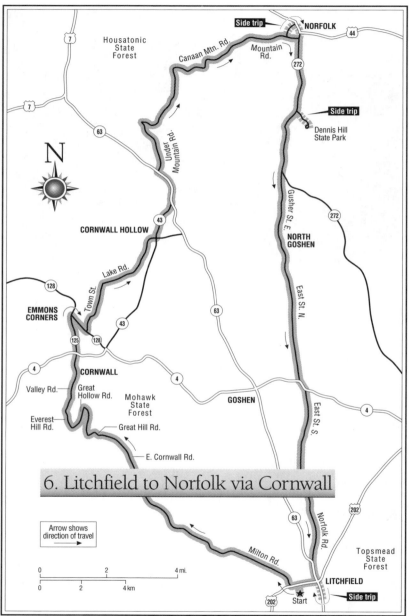

6. Litchfield to Norfolk via Cornwall

Housatonic State Forest

Canaan Mtn. Rd.

Mountain Rd.

NORFOLK

Side trip

44

272

Under Mountain Rd.

Dennis Hill State Park

Side trip

63

7

7

N

CORNWALL HOLLOW

43

Lake Rd.

Gusher St. E.

NORTH GOSHEN

272

128

Town St.

EMMONS CORNERS

43

63

East St. N.

125

128

4

CORNWALL

Valley Rd.

Great Hollow Rd.

Mohawk State Forest

4

GOSHEN

4

Everest Hill Rd.

Great Hill Rd.

E. Cornwall Rd.

East St. S.

Arrow shows direction of travel

Milton Rd.

63

202

Norfolk Rd.

Topsmead State Forest

0   2   4 mi.
0   2   4 km

202

Start

LITCHFIELD

Side trip

Paul Woodward, © 2000 The Countryman Press

6
Litchfield to Norfolk via Cornwall

Distance: *47.9 miles*
Terrain: *Varied terrain with one challenging climb up Canaan Mountain;*
   2.5 miles of dirt road
Difficulty: *Strenuous*
Recommended bicycle: *Touring/road bike*

The postcard village of Litchfield is many people's idea of quintessential colonial New England: broad tree-lined avenues graced with historic mansions and a common laid out in the 1770s. The gleaming white facade of the 1829 First Congregational Church on the edge of the green is one of the most photographed in New England.

Historians also agree that it is one of New England's best-preserved 18th-century villages. The entire town center is a National Historic Landmark. The grand old homes along North and South Streets were built by merchants and ship owners made wealthy by trade with England and China; some of these homes are open to the public during Litchfield's annual house tours. Among them are the nation's first law school and school for girls, and taverns and inns that hosted George Washington, Alexander Hamilton, the Marquis de Lafayette, and other heroes of the American Revolution.

Litchfield was prominent in the politics of the colonial and federalist eras. The village was home to elite aristocratic families who supported the Revolution and was the birthplace of abolitionist writer Harriet Beecher Stowe and Ethan Allen.

High on this list of freethinkers is Oliver Wolcott Sr., signer of the Declaration of Independence, member of the Continental Congress, and governor of Connecticut. During the heady days of the Revolution, a statue of King George III was smuggled to Litchfield in an oxcart. In an apple orchard behind Wolcott's 1753 home, the bronze was melted down and turned into bullets by Wolcott's family members and fellow patriots, so the redcoats "would have melted majesty fired at them."

Col. Benjamin Tallmadge, one of Washington's most trusted aides, built a gambrel-roofed mansion here in 1775, where military leaders met during the war. Tapping Reeve opened the nation's first law school on South Street in 1784. Its distinguished roster of students included Aaron Burr (Reeve was married to Burr's sister, Sally), Horace Mann, John C. Calhoun, Supreme Court justices, and 130 members of Congress. Harriet Beecher Stowe was born in the family homestead on North Street in 1775. Also on North Street is the site of the country's first academy for girls, founded by Sarah Pierce in 1792.

The thickly forested upland town of Cornwall is actually six secluded hamlets, blessedly untouched by progress, perhaps because they are nestled into some of the state's steepest terrain. A small number of New Yorkers, mostly writers and artists, began visiting in the 1920s, and the Cornwalls—North Cornwall, Cornwall Village (sometimes called Cornwall Plain), and East Cornwall are on this tour—continue to attract summer visitors and urban refugees to its deep hills and peaceful valleys. Autumn foliage is spectacular here, as the hickories, oaks, and maples light up the hills.

The quiet beauty of Norfolk lured wealthy New York families in the mid-1800s to build opulent summer "cottages" in its cool green hills. One of these magnificent estates is the site of an acclaimed international chamber music festival and the Yale Summer School of Music. Norfolk is also known for its romantic inns and leafy village green, considered among the prettiest in the state.

Directions for the Ride

This tour leads you through some of the most beautiful scenery in the Litchfield Hills. Begin at the Cycle Loft in the Litchfield Commons shopping area on US 202, just west of the Litchfield green.

0.0 From the parking lot, turn left onto Bantam Road (US 202).

0.2 At the traffic light, turn right onto Milton Road.

0.5 Bear left on Milton Road.

This gently rolling road cuts through a pastoral landscape of farms, fields, and stone walls.

3.1 At Bunnell Farm, bear right to continue on Milton Road.

3.2 Follow Milton Road as it turns left.

The sleepy hamlet of Milton has the idyllic feel of a place long forgotten by time. The green-shuttered congregational church, a handful of carefully preserved homes, and the tiny white Milton Hall are linked by an expanse of green at its center. In the 19th century, Milton was bustling with five sawmills, two gristmills, an ironworks, two shoemakers, and six schoolhouses. Today it's a mere shadow of its former self, a place where modernity seems an oddity.

5.1 Bear right onto Milton Road.

Beautiful historic homesteads, including a 1750 tollhouse, line the way out of the village.

5.6 Bear right onto East Cornwall Road.

After passing a sizable farm, the road enters the woods.

8.4 Begin descending Great Hill Road.

Use extreme caution on this very steep, winding descent.

9.6 At the bottom of the hill, turn left onto Great Hollow Road.

This flat stretch of road leads toward the village of Cornwall.

10.4 Turn right onto Everest Hill Road.

11.0 Turn right onto Valley Road.

A ribbon of road cuts through this broad valley on the edge of Cornwall. Just before the village on Essex Hill Road is a beautiful stretch of ancient forest called Cathedral in the Pines. It was one of the largest virgin forests to survive the widespread deforestation of the 19th and early 20th centuries. The stands of white pine were nearly obliterated in a 1989 tornado, but visitors can see the regrowth of these towering giants taking place in this peaceful sanctuary that receives few visitors.

12.5 In Cornwall, turn right onto Pine Street.

Take some time to explore the side streets of this tiny village to see its charming homes and churches. The Foreign Mission School

Shops along the historic Litchfield green.

was founded here in 1817 to educate Hawaiian and Native American missionaries. Henry Obookiah, a converted priest from the Sandwich Islands, died of typhus while a student at the school. His writings inspired missionaries to journey to Hawaii; these island expeditions inspired James Michener to write a novel. The school closed in 1826, following community outrage over the marriage of two Native American students to local girls.

12.9 *At the stop sign, go straight across Cemetery Hill (CT 4) onto Grange Hall Road (CT 125 North).*

14.2 *Make a sharp right turn uphill at the stop sign onto Sharon-Goshen Turnpike (CT 128).*

14.9 *Turn left onto Town Street.*

Check out the white marker on the corner, pointing up Town Street to North Cornwall. It designates former and existing historic sites in Cornwall's six villages.

In about a mile, you'll reach the village of North Cornwall, marked only by a handful of old homes and the 1826 North Cornwall Congregational Meeting House set on a broad plain.

16.5 *Bear right onto Lake Road.*

You'll descend through woods past Cream Hill Lake and an old homestead tucked into a beautiful open valley.

18.5 *At the stop sign, turn left onto Cornwall Hollow Road (CT 43).*

20.1 *Turn left onto Hollenbeck Road (CT 63).*

This road takes you across the Canaan town line and the Hollenbeck River.

21.3 *Turn right onto Under Mountain Road.*

This road opens onto a small farming valley in the shadow of Canaan Mountain.

22.7 *Continue straight on Under Mountain Road (Cobble Road goes left).*

23.0 *Turn right onto Canaan Mountain Road.*

Begin the tour's toughest climb, a strenuous 1.5-mile ascent of Canaan Mountain through Great Mountain Forest, a 6,000-acre experimental tract maintained by the Yale School of Forestry, and Housatonic State Forest.

25.5 *Bear right onto Wangum Road.*

This road narrows and turns to dirt for about 2.5 miles, hugging the remote shore of Wangum Lake before heading east into the woods toward Norfolk.

The road returns to pavement at the Norfolk town line, becomes Mountain Road, and descends toward the village. You'll see some of the genteel country estates for which Norfolk is well known.

29.1 *At the next two stop signs, continue straight on Mountain Road.*

30.0 *Turn right onto Litchfield Road (CT 272).*

Side Trip One: Turn left for a short jaunt to Norfolk's charming village green. The Ellen Battel Stoeckel estate has been called the "Lenox of Connecticut" for its renowned summer chamber music festival and concerts by the Yale Summer School of Music.

Side Trip Two: About 2 miles down Litchfield Road on the left is Dennis Hill State Park, marked by a small brown sign. If you are up to the challenge, a climb through a mixed hardwood forest will reward you at the top with panoramic views of the surrounding hills. At the top Dr. Frederick S. Dennis built himself a lavish bungalow in 1908, where he entertained such illustrious guests as President Taft and Andrew Carnegie. The 240-acre estate of the noted New York surgeon was given to the state in 1935. From the observation pavilion on the roof of the house, you can see Haystack Mountain on the other side of town, Mount Greylock in the Berkshires, and the mountains of southern New Hampshire.

34.3 *Bear right onto Goshen East Street.*

After a short, steep climb, this country road rolls past woodland and farms. As you cross the Goshen town line, it becomes East Street North.

41.0 *Turn left onto Torrington Road (CT 4).*

41.2 *Turn right onto East Street South.*

44.2 *At the stop sign, head straight on Norfolk Road.*

In about 2 miles, you'll pass the campus of the Forman School, which opened in 1930 for boys with special learning needs. The childhood residence of Harriet Beecher Stowe was originally at the site; the historic structure has been sold, disassembled, and put in storage while its new owner finds a site for it. Forman is now a coed school on a campus designed to blend into its historic neighborhood.

46.8 **At the stop sign, turn left onto North Street (CT 63).**

Some of Litchfield's most spectacular mansions line this road to the green.

47.3 **At the traffic light, turn right onto US 202.**

The Litchfield green is straight ahead. For a short side trip, cross the green and explore the historic homes, including the Tapping Reeve House and Law School, on South Street. The Litchfield Historical Society Museum on the corner of East and South Streets has exhibits on Litchfield history as well as early American paintings, furniture, and decorative arts. A collection of boutiques and cafés lines the edge of the green on West Street.

47.9 **The tour ends at the Litchfield Commons on the left.**

Bicycle Shops

Cycle Loft, 25 Commons Drive (US 202), Litchfield; 860-567-1713

Tommy's Bicycles & Fitness, 40 East Main Street (US 202), Torrington; 860-482-3571

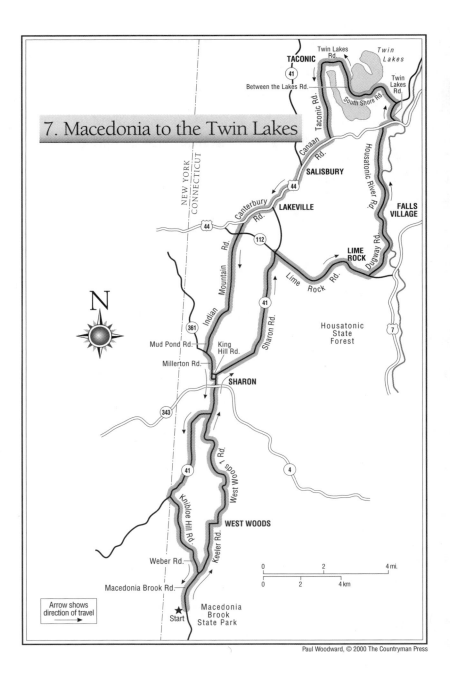

7. Macedonia to the Twin Lakes

NEW YORK
CONNECTICUT

TACONIC
41

Twin Lakes Rd.

Twin Lakes

Between the Lakes Rd.

Twin Lakes Rd.

South Shore Rd.

Canaan Taconic Rd.

Housatonic River Rd.

SALISBURY
44

Canterbury Rd.

LAKEVILLE

44

112

FALLS VILLAGE

LIME ROCK

Dugway Rd.

Lime Rock Rd.

N

Mountain Rd.

Indian

361

41

Sharon Rd.

Housatonic State Forest

7

Mud Pond Rd.

King Hill Rd.

Millerton Rd.

SHARON

343

West Woods Rd.

4

41

WEST WOODS

Knibloe Hill Rd.

Keeler Rd.

Weber Rd.

Macedonia Brook Rd.

| 0 | | 2 | | 4 mi. |
| 0 | | 2 | 4 km | |

★ Start

Macedonia Brook State Park

Arrow shows
direction of travel

Paul Woodward, © 2000 The Countryman Press

7

Macedonia to the Twin Lakes

Distance: *50.8 miles*
Terrain: *Rolling hills, including about 13 miles of dirt roads*
Difficulty: *Moderate to strenuous*
Recommended bicycle: *Hybrid*

This tour passes through some of the most rural back roads in Connecticut. You'll probably be the only person on these largely forgotten dirt country lanes, which link Kent to Sharon and follow a peaceful lazy stretch of the Housatonic River through Salisbury.

Life along these dirt roads seems to have slipped out of the mainstream of 20th-century America. You'll ride through an old-fashioned landscape of historic homesteads, some lovingly restored, others worn by centuries of harsh New England weather.

Even the paved routes connecting these secluded areas are spectacular. CT 41 through Sharon has lovely panoramas on both sides of the road, a patchwork of farm fields rising to the foothills of the Berkshires. The heart and soul of this area is on the farms tucked into hidden valleys and on hilltops.

The Housatonic River cuts a swath through this rural corner of the state, carrying the cool waters of the Berkshires through western Connecticut to Long Island Sound, flowing past rural scenes that few cars pass.

The ride begins in Kent's Macedonia Brook State Park, a 2,300-acre tract of rugged terrain on the New York border. It heads north to the charming village of Sharon, which flourished in the 18th century by manufacturing everything from tools and stoves to wooden mousetraps. Many working farms still exist in Sharon's outlying hills.

The summits of the state's loftiest peaks—Riga, Bear, and Lion's

Head—stand sentinel over the upscale village of Salisbury, a popular haven for weekend visitors.

Much of the natural beauty of Salisbury's Twin Lakes remains unspoiled, thanks to the foresight of the area's first landowners and developers at the turn of the 20th century.

When settlers first came to the area, only a few families farmed the shores of Lake Washining and Lake Washinee. The railroad brought the first influx of summer visitors in the 1870s, and a seasonal community of rustic cottages and camps grew along the lakeshores. One of the first lodges, built by John O'Hara late in the 19th century, is still open as a beach and marina.

Directions for the Ride

Macedonia Brook State Park is in the Macedonia section of Kent, about 2 miles west of Main Street on CT 341. Turn right onto Macedonia Brook Road, following the state park signs to the camp office, about 1 mile into the park. Drive past this log building and turn left into the dirt parking lot at the trailhead to Cobble Mountain.

0.0 *Turn left out of the parking lot, cross a small wooden bridge, and head up Macedonia Brook Road.*

This pretty dirt road follows Macedonia Brook through the woods. You'll soon pass a massive, intricately crafted dry-laid stone wall, the handiwork of the Civilian Conservation Corps. The wall was completed in 1935, part of President Roosevelt's initiative that gave employment to young men during the Great Depression. Workers received $30 a month, with $25 sent home to their families. The CCC helped build and maintain state and national parks around the country.

1.3 *Cross another small bridge, then make a sharp right turn onto Keeler Road.*

This secluded dirt road rises away from the park boundary, passing a few scattered homes and abandoned farm buildings as it winds gently north through dense woods into Sharon.

2.9 *At the stop sign, continue following Keeler Road as it turns sharply to the right and becomes paved.*

You'll pass a horse farm on the right as you make the turn.

3.4 At the stop sign, turn left onto West Woods Road #1.

Look carefully at the signposts at this junction of dirt roads. Be sure not to turn right onto West Woods Road #2.

This secluded narrow road winds, mostly downhill, and becomes paved at the end. You'll pass by a couple of old homesteads surrounded by hayfields and forest.

7.6 Follow West Woods Road #1 as it turns sharply to the right.

On this flat hilltop road you'll begin to see Sharon's trademark pastoral views.

7.9 At the stop sign, go straight onto South Main Street (CT 41) into the village of Sharon.

At 18 Main Street, across from the congregational church, stands a stately 1775 redbrick Colonial, built by illustrious Sharon resident and Revolutionary War veteran Ebenezer Gay. It is now the Gay-Hoyt House Museum (860-364-5688), operated by the Sharon Historical Society.

8.8 Go through the center of Sharon on Main Street.

Just past the green is a shopping plaza with a grocery store, your last opportunity to pick up supplies until you reach Salisbury.

14.2 At the stop sign, turn right onto Lime Rock Road (CT 112).

The sloping manicured lawns on the right are those of the prestigious Hotchkiss School, whose Georgian brick buildings are modeled after those in Harvard Yard. Past the school, and descend smoothly through horse country into the tiny village of Lime Rock. When you arrive at the outfield entrance of Lime Rock Raceway, slow down and look for your next turn.

18.2 At the stone Trinity Episcopal Church, turn left onto Dugway Road.

About a mile down this quiet, shady back road you'll begin to catch glimpses of a wide, flat-water section of the Housatonic River between the trees. When you hear the river's Class I and II rapids, you'll know you're near the Falls Village power plant, an imposing redbrick building standing sentry across the river. This is a popular access point for the legions of paddlers that travel

The Housatonic River near Falls Village.

the river downstream to West Cornwall and Kent.

20.6 *With the iron bridge to your right, turn left and then immediately right onto Falls Road.*

During periods of high water, you may see expert paddlers negotiate this turbulent and dangerous stretch of Class V rapids known as "Rattlesnake" from the foot of Great Falls to the iron bridge.

20.9 *At the Y-intersection, bear right onto Housatonic River Road.*

This road soon becomes unpaved and cuts through a rural farming valley on the river.

24.1 *Turn right onto Canaan Road (US 44).*

24.6 *Turn left onto Twin Lakes Road.*

Look for a large, white-columned house and a historic burying ground at this intersection.

25.4 *Bear left, remaining on Twin Lakes Road.*

Begin a moderate climb into the woods.

26.2 *Turn left on South Shore Road.*

Watch carefully for the white signpost marking this very narrow one-lane road. It twists through the woods past summer cottages on beautiful Lake Washining (East Twin Lake) and eventually turns to dirt.

27.2 **At the end of South Shore Road, turn right on Between the Lakes Road.**

This dirt road, as the name implies, traverses a slim median between the lakes.

27.7 **At the stop sign, turn left onto Twin Lakes Road.**

Ride along a series of dips toward the brown-shingled post office in Taconic.

29.2 **Bear left at the Y-junction on the tiny green in Taconic onto Taconic Road.**

Follow the white sign pointing to Salisbury, Lakeville, and US 44.

31.9 **Turn right onto Canaan Road (US 44) toward Salisbury.**

Salisbury's Main Street is flanked by vintage homes, boutiques, and eateries ranging from delis to gourmet inns.

Side Trip: This extremely challenging but rewarding trip (not recommended for road bikes) takes you into the northwest corner's highest elevations. At the Salisbury Town Hall, turn onto Washnee Street. In about 0.5 mile, turn onto the narrow, gravel Mount Riga Road, which you will climb for 2.6 miles before making a sharp right turn onto Mount Washington Road. In about 2.8 miles, you will come across a sign designating a hiking trail. In about 1 mile, this will reach the Appalachian Trail. From here you can retrace your route to Salisbury.

35.2 **At the blinking light in Lakeville, bear right onto Millerton Road (US 44).**

36.4 **Turn left onto Indian Mountain Road.**

You'll pedal across CT 112 and past the Indian Mountain School campus before crossing the Sharon town line. Here the road changes to Mudge Pond Road and passes along its scenic namesake pond.

41.3 **At the stop sign, turn left onto Millerton Road (CT 361) and follow it into Sharon.**

At the end of CT 361, make a quick left and then right to bring you back to the village green.

41.8 At the stop sign, go straight onto South Main Street (CT 41).

The granite clock tower here was built by Italian stonemasons who came to Sharon in the late 19th century to construct elegant mansions for its prosperous residents.

42.7 Follow CT 41 as it bears right, becomes Amenia-Union Road, and heads toward the New York state line.

46.3 At the stop sign at Hitchcock Corners (Amenia Union), turn left onto NY 2 and follow the sign to Kent.

46.4 Take the first left onto Knibloe Hill Road.

Begin a climb here that varies from moderate to steep, passing a few weathered barns before winding into the woods.

48.4 Bear right onto Weber Road.

The only signpost here is for Caray Road, which goes to the left. Weber Road leads back into Macedonia Brook State Park.

49.5 Bear left and then quickly right onto Macedonia Brook Road.

50.8 End the ride at the Cobble Mountain trailhead.

Bicycle Shops

The Bike Doctor & Sports Center, 97 Church Street (US 44), Canaan; 860-824-5577

Bike Express, 73 Bridge Street (CT 67 and US 202), New Milford; 860-354-1466

8

The Litchfield Hills:
A Two-Day Tour

Distance: 114.6 miles total; 56.7 miles (Day One) and 57.9 miles (Day Two)

Terrain: Gradual to steep hills connected by rolling terrain

Difficulty: Strenuous

Recommended bicycle: Touring/road bike

The absence of interstates or major cities in the Northwest Corner is a product of its hilly terrain, which deterred much of the 19th-century industrialization that swept through other parts of the state. As a result, the colonial villages that you will visit on this 2-day ride are much as they were centuries ago. All along the way, you'll pass many of the homesteads built by the earliest settlers who came to farm these rocky lands. Quiet hamlets like Washington, Warren, and Merryall are still home to rolling countryside dotted with pastures, horse farms, silos, and clapboard farmhouses. In Sharon, Roxbury, and Salisbury, livestock graze in lush fields bordered by the forests that have reclaimed much of these farm fields in the last century. Many of Litchfield County's former dairy farms have been converted to country estates with guest houses and artist's studios, a metamorphosis that has become characteristic of these hills in the last couple of decades.

To get to the northernmost reaches of this ride, you will follow the Housatonic River upstream for several miles, passing West Cornwall and its landmark covered bridge before heading through the Salmon Kill Valley into Salisbury.

In the 1700s, Salisbury and Lakeville had the nation's leading iron mines and forges. Connecticut's first blast furnace was owned by Ethan Allen, leader of the Green Mountain Boys, who captured Fort Ticon-

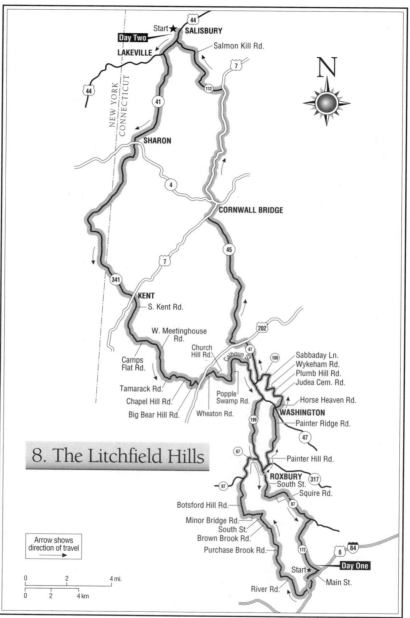

N

Start ★ SALISBURY
44
Day Two
LAKEVILLE
Salmon Kill Rd.
7
44
112
NEW YORK
CONNECTICUT
41
SHARON
4
CORNWALL BRIDGE
45
7
341
KENT
S. Kent Rd.
W. Meetinghouse Rd.
202
Church Hill Rd.
Calhoun St.
47
109
Sabbaday Ln.
Camps Flat Rd.
Wykeham Rd.
Plumb Hill Rd.
Judea Cem. Rd.
Tamarack Rd.
Popple Swamp Rd.
Horse Heaven Rd.
Chapel Hill Rd.
WASHINGTON
Big Bear Hill Rd.
Wheaton Rd.
Painter Ridge Rd.
199
47
8. The Litchfield Hills
67
Painter Hill Rd.
ROXBURY
317
67
South St.
Squire Rd.
Botsford Hill Rd.
67
Minor Bridge Rd.
South St.
Brown Brook Rd.
Purchase Brook Rd.
172
6
84
Start ★
Day One
Arrow shows direction of travel
River Rd.
Main St.

0   2   4 mi.
0   2   4 km

Paul Woodward, © 2000 The Countryman Press

deroga from the British. In one 7-month period during the Revolutionary War, Allen's forge in Lakeville produced 116 tons of cannon and 38 tons of shot and balls.

Blast furnaces around Salisbury were also busy during the Civil War; one of the most notable was the Mount Riga furnace, built around 1810 on a wilderness plateau above Salisbury. A hillside community of about 100 families sprung up around the Mount Riga furnace, but when it closed in 1847 the population vanished.

The Mount Riga furnace produced anchors for the navy during the War of 1812. To test its durability, a 20-ton anchor would be dropped from a 100-foot tower. If it didn't break, the navy would use it. The whole town would gather for this spectacle.

The triphammer used to shape hot iron into anchors sits in front of Salisbury Town Hall, a reminder that in the 18th century this upscale village was highly industrialized. Today it's hard to imagine that smoke, noise, and pollution churned out by forges and furnaces filled these quiet hills, where artists, celebrities, and wealthy urbanites now retreat.

Day One

Distance: *56.7 miles*
Terrain: *Rolling hills with several steep climbs; some flat stretches along the Housatonic River*

Accommodations Near the Start of the Ride

The Heritage, Heritage Village off US 6, Southbury; 1-800-932-3466

Mill at Pomperaug, 29 Pomperaug Road, Woodbury; 203-263-4566

Merryvale, 1204 Main Street South, Woodbury; 203-266-0800

The tour begins in Southbury just off I-84 at exit 14. Follow the tourist information signs that lead to the Southbury Travel Center, where there is parking in a gated lot.

You can pick up supplies in Southbury, and several of the villages have general stores and delis. Class Cycles, on Main Street North, is the only bike shop on the tour.

0.0 Turn left out of the travel center onto Main Street South.
This flat road will follow I-84 for nearly a mile before curving to the left and crossing over the interstate.

0.9 At the stop sign, turn right onto Fish Rock Road.

This will cross the highway again before heading toward the Housatonic River.

2.6 Bear right onto River Road (to the left is a steel bridge at the Newtown town line).

Follow this wide, lazy stretch of the Housatonic River upstream.

4.8 Turn right onto Purchase Brook Road.

Here you leave the river and get your first taste of the Litchfield Hills as you climb past Mitchell Farm, in operation since 1759.

6.5 At the stop sign, bear left to continue on Purchase Brook Road.

Another steep 0.5-mile climb begins here.

7.7 Turn left onto Brown Brook Road at the next stop sign.

This leads to a fast, curving descent and turns into South Street when you cross the Roxbury town line at the bottom.

9.4 Turn left onto Minor Bridge Road.

After descending for about a mile, cross a bridge over a boulder-strewn gorge in the Shepaug River, popular with swimmers in summer. After the bridge, begin a steep 1-mile climb.

10.7 Turn right onto Town Line Road.

This strenuous climb continues for another 0.5 mile, leading to a peaceful ribbon of farm road straddling the border of Bridgewater and Roxbury. It seems as if time stopped on this ridge, thanks in part to the conservation efforts of the Bridgewater Land Trust.

13.5 Turn right onto Baker Road (CT 67).

This follows the Shepaug River and then winds uphill toward the genteel village of Roxbury. In the 19th century, residents hoped to make their fortunes when it was rumored that there was silver in the hills high above the Shepaug River. Instead, the town prospered from its garnet and granite mines; the latter supplied the materials for New York's Grand Central Station and Brooklyn Bridge.

16.5 At the stop sign in the center of the village, go straight onto

White Hollow Farms in the Lime Rock section of Salisbury.

Church Street (CT 67). When CT 67 turns right toward South-bury, continue straight onto Good Hill Road (CT 317) toward Woodbury.

17.0 *Turn left onto Painter Hill Road.*

Across Good Hill Road you will see Maple Bank Farm, a produce and flower farm market. This pretty back road climbs to a hilltop farm.

19.2 *At the stop sign, turn left onto Painter Ridge Road, following the sign to Washington.*

(Painter Hill Road goes to the right here, toward Woodbury.) This road follows an open ridge into Washington.

20.9 *At the stop sign, cross Nichols Hill Road and continue straight on Painter Ridge Road.*

21.4 *At the bottom of Painter Ridge Road, bear right on a narrow* *side road, just before the stop sign. At this stop sign, cross Woodbury Road (CT 47) onto Horse Heaven Road.*

22.3 At the Y-intersection, bear left onto Judea Cemetery Road (unmarked).

22.9 At the stop sign, turn right onto Bell Hill Road.

Climb a short hill and then make a straight descent to another stop sign.

23.4 Turn left onto Wykeham Road.

The International College of Hospitality Management is on the left.

24.0 Turn right onto Sabbaday Lane.

At a quiet Y-intersection, bear right (Mallory Brook Road is to the left) and descend to a single-lane bridge.

25.0 Turn left onto Blackville Road (CT 109; unmarked).

26.1 At the stop sign, turn right onto Bee Brook Road (CT 47) and follow it to the end.

29.0 Turn left onto Litchfield Turnpike (US 202).

29.6 Turn right onto Flirtation Avenue.

30.2 At the stop sign, turn right onto Lake Road (CT 45).

Follow the east shore of picturesque Lake Waramaug into the town of Warren. The road rises into the hills as it leads away from the lake, mixing short climbs with flat stretches.

33.4 At the stop sign, bear left onto CT 341/CT 45.

35.0 Bear right onto Cornwall Road (CT 45).

Perched on a hill above this intersection is the magnificent 1820 Warren Congregational Church. The white clapboard Warren's General Store on the left has sandwiches, drinks, and groceries. As you cross into Cornwall, this becomes Warren Hill Road and descends toward the Housatonic River valley.

39.9 Bear right onto Kent Road (US 7 North).

In the village of Cornwall Bridge, turn left to continue on US 7 North, cross the Housatonic River into Sharon, and immediately bear right, staying on US 7 as it turns into River Road. The Housatonic drifts and churns along this scenic stretch near Housatonic Meadows State Park. In about 6 miles, watch for West Cornwall's red covered bridge spanning the river.

50.1 *Turn left onto Lime Rock Road (CT 112).*

52.0 *Turn right onto Salmon Kill Road.*

This narrow, serpentine road cuts through bucolic Salmon Kill Valley.

56.2 *At the stop sign, turn right onto Canaan Road (US 44) in the village of Salisbury.*

This day's ride ends at the village green, at the junction of CT 41 and US 44, in front of the White Hart Inn.

Accommodations in the Area

White Hart Inn, on the village green (CT 41 and US 44), Salisbury; 860-435-0030

Iron Masters Motor Inne, 229 Main Street (CT 41 and US 44), Lakeville; 860-435-9844

Ragamont Inn, 8 Main Street (CT 41 and US 44), Salisbury; 860-435-2372

Alice's Bed & Breakfast, 267 Main Street (CT 41 and US 44), Lakeville; 860-435-8808

Other Travel Information

Litchfield Hills Travel Council; 860-567-4506

Covered Bridge B&B Reservation Service; 860-542-5944

Nutmeg Bed and Breakfast Agency; 860-236-6698 or 1-800-727-7592

Day Two

Distance: *57.9 miles*
Terrain: *Rolling to hilly*

0.0 *Leave Salisbury by heading west on Main Street (CT 41/US 44) toward Lakeville.*

1.8 *At the blinking light in Lakeville, follow CT 41 to the left as it splits from US 44.*

2.1 Facing the church, bear right onto CT 41.

3.4 At the stop sign, continue straight on CT 41 through Sharon.

This rural community was made wealthy by the Yankee ingenuity of its residents, who invented wooden mousetraps, produced cigars, and raised silkworms on the mulberry trees lining Main Street. The red and gray granite clock tower at the lower end of Main Street was created by talented Italian stonemasons in 1885, who were imported here to build the elegant mansions seen today.

13.3 On the Connecticut/New York border, turn left onto NY 2, following the sign for Kent.

16.2 Turn left onto Kent Road (NY 3).

17.1 Turn left, staying on NY 3.

Crossing back into Connecticut, NY 3 turns into Macedonia Road (CT 341), passing the village of Macedonia and the dignified campus of the Kent School. Macedonia Brook State Park has many wooded, brookside picnic tables.

23.2 At the traffic light, go straight onto CT 341.

Side Trip: Kent was once famous for its iron forges and blast furnaces. The Sloane-Stanley Museum on Main Street features the remains of an early iron forge. Main Street is also packed with galleries, boutiques, and cafés.

23.8 Bear right onto South Kent Road (CT 341 goes to the left).

Enjoy this flat, easy section of road.

26.8 Turn left onto Camp Flats Road.

Moderate, undulating climbs are linked with flat sections.

29.4 Bear right onto West Meetinghouse Road.

Rolling hills lead to a steep descent.

30.6 Turn left onto Tamarack Road.

31.4 Bear right onto Chapel Hill Road.

This road takes you into the heart of the quiet hamlet of Merryall. The Merryall Chapel, c. 1890, is a rural roadside church; just up the road is the Merryall Center for the Arts, housed in a tiny red cottage.

33.0 *Turn left onto Big Bear Hill Road.*

There is a short but extremely steep climb as you turn onto this road, then a longer, precipitous descent on the other side.

34.0 *Turn left onto Litchfield Road (US 202).*

34.7 *Turn right onto Wheaton Road.*

Look for this turn just after you pass a cemetery on the right.

35.4 *Turn right onto Upper Church Hill Road.*

This long, winding climb will bring you past some of Washington's hilltop farms.

37.0 *Turn left onto Popple Swamp Road.*

38.3 *Turn right onto Scofield Hill Road for a short time. At a stop sign go straight onto Kinney Hill Road.*

38.5 *At the stop sign, turn right onto Calhoun Street.*

Calhoun Street has some of this 18th-century town's most historic buildings, including the Averill homestead, c. 1746.

39.6 *Bear right to continue on Calhoun Street.*

39.7 *At the stop sign, turn left to continue on Calhoun Street (Ives Road, which is marked, is to the right).*

40.3 *Turn left onto Baldwin Hill Road.*

41.0 *In the center of Washington Depot, continue straight on CT 47 as it climbs Green Hill to the Washington green.*

The centerpiece of this hilltop village is the impressive 1801 First Congregational Church. The green, laid out in the 1740s, is surrounded by handsome antique homes and an old-fashioned post office and general store, which is now a deli.

42.1 *Turn right onto Roxbury Road (CT 199).*

The Institute for American Indian Studies, on Curtis Road (860-868-0518), has impressive historical exhibits on the history of Connecticut's woodland Native Americans, a 17th-century replicated Algonkian village in the woods behind the museum, and a simulated archaeological site.

46.8 *At the stop sign, turn left onto CT 67.*

47.6 *In Roxbury, bear right at the small green (CT 67 goes left). At the stop sign, turn right and then immediately left onto South Street.*

Passing through Roxbury's quiet historic district, notice the 18th- and 19th-century homes surrounded by scenic open fields. Many of these charming, carefully restored homes flank South Street, with architectural styles running the gamut from center-chimney Colonials and late Greek Revivals to a 19th-century shoe factory converted into a private residence.

48.2 *Continue straight at the stop sign.*

49.5 *Turn left onto Squire Road.*

50.9 *Turn right onto CT 67.*

53.5 *At the stop sign, go right onto South Britain Road (CT 172).*

The roadside village of South Britain has little more than a stately 1825 church and Victorian-style clapboard general store facing each other across South Britain Road. There is also a tiny green-shingled library and a cluster of Revolutionary-era homes strung along the Pomperaug River.

57.8 *At the traffic light, turn right onto Main Street South, then left into the second driveway at Southbury Travel Center, where the tour ends.*

Bicycle Shops

Bike Express, 73 Bridge Street (CT 67 and US 202), New Milford; 860-354-1466

Class Cycles, 77 Main Street North (CT 67), Southbury; 203-264-4708

9
Winchester Center to Norfolk via Colebrook

Distance: *44.2 miles*
Terrain: *Rolling hills with a couple of steep climbs; two very short dirt roads*
Difficulty: *Strenuous*
Recommended bicycle: *Touring/road bike*

The tiny Winchester green is a hilltop convergence of a few rural country roads flanked by Colonial buildings and farms surrounded by wide, sloping meadows. Next to the neat, white Winchester Congregational Church sits a private home that has served the village in turn as a post office, gristmill, and general store. Today it is the Kerosene Lamp Museum (860-379-2612), which houses one man's collection of 500 kerosene hanging and standing lamps dating from 1856 to 1880.

Winchester has a secluded, little-used gem of a park that makes a perfect rest stop on the tour. Just after you crest 1,457-foot Platt Hill, look for the entrance to Platt Hill State Park, which has wooded picnic sites and views of Highland Lake and the surrounding hills.

Tucked into verdant hills of second- and third-growth forests is Colebrook, considered one of New England's best preserved post-Revolutionary villages. The Colebrook Store was built in 1812 for brothers Martin and Solomon Rockwell, whose prominent family owned an iron forge. It has been open ever since, making it Connecticut's oldest continually operating general store. Its columns, original pine floorboards, pressed tin ceiling, and woodstove are just as they were in the 19th century. Just past the Colebrook Store on the left is the Samuel Rockwell House, c. 1767, one of the village's first homes, and on the west side of the church is the Martin Rockwell House. The Colebrook Inn, now the

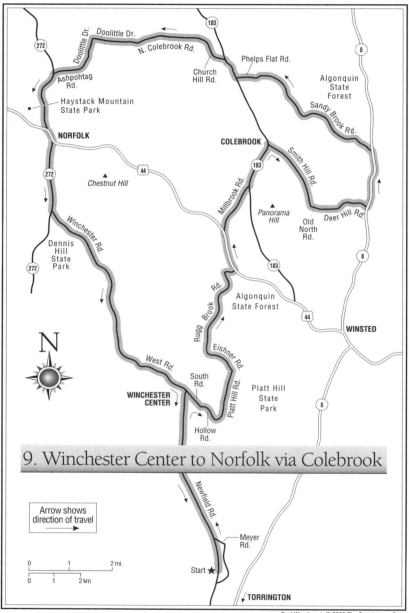

272
Doolittle Dr.
Doolittle Dr.
183
N. Colebrook Rd.
Phelps Flat Rd.
8
Church Hill Rd.
Algonquin State Forest
Ashpohtag Rd.
Sandy Brook Rd.
Haystack Mountain State Park
NORFOLK
COLEBROOK
44
183
Smith Hill Rd.
Chestnut Hill
272
Millbrook Rd.
Panorama Hill
Deer Hill Rd.
8
Dennis Hill State Park
Old North Rd.
272
183
Winchester Rd.
Algonquin State Forest
44
WINSTED
Rugg Brook Rd.
West Rd.
Eishner Rd.
8
South Rd.
Platt Hill Rd.
WINCHESTER CENTER
Platt Hill State Park
Hollow Rd.

9. Winchester Center to Norfolk via Colebrook

N

Arrow shows direction of travel

Newfield Rd.

0   1   2 mi.
0   1   2 km

Meyer Rd.

Start ★

TORRINGTON

town hall and historical society, used to feed and lodge travelers passing through the village on the New Haven Turnpike.

Colebrook's population peaked in the pre–Civil War era when woolen industries, tanneries, and a scythe factory sprang up in the hills. In the 1860s, when the local population swelled with mill and factory workers, the village supported six general stores. By the 1900s Colebrook was primarily a summer colony, and today the Colebrook Store is the town's only remaining business.

To the west, Norfolk's spot high in Litchfield County's upland hills has earned it the nickname of the "icebox of Connecticut." This cool climate made it a popular summer retreat for high society in the late 19th century. Many of the elaborate summer homes built by railroad, steel, and mining magnates in the late 1800s have been carefully preserved; some are now charming inns and B&Bs. The village's cultural heritage is centered on the esteemed Norfolk Music Festival at the Ellen Battell Stoeckel estate, which also hosts the Yale Summer School of Music.

Directions for the Ride

The ride does not start near any food stores, so you may want to pick up supplies in Torrington. The first place to stop will be the general store in Colebrook, about 14 miles into the tour.

Start from the small parking area at East Branch Dam on Newfield Road in Torrington, 1.2 miles north of the junction of Newfield and Winsted Roads in the city's north end. Torrington can be reached from US 8, US 202, or CT 4.

0.0 *From the parking area, turn left onto Newfield Road. This long, gradual climb with some level sections will take you into Winchester Center.*

4.6 *At the Winchester green, turn right onto South Road.*

Winchester was incorporated in 1771, then virtually forgotten when a newly built turnpike bypassed the hilltop in 1799. A clock-making industry grew in a new valley settlement to the east called Winsted, which is still the town's business center.

5.2 *Turn left onto Hollow Road, a short, hard-packed dirt road passing by a small pond.*

To avoid the dirt road, continue on South Road and take the next left on Platt Hill Road.

5.7   At the stop sign, turn left onto Platt Hill Road.

On the right you will pass a c. 1815 one-room schoolhouse, which local children attended until the turn of the 20th century. A former teacher then purchased it and turned it over to a preservation group. The Little Red Schoolhouse Association (860-626-0326) opens the school to visitors at select times each year. The inside of the little school looks much as it did when students attended it, with period desks and chairs and the stove that kept them warm through harsh New England winters.

7.1   Bear left onto Laurel Way (Eishner Road).

In early June, Winchester plays host to the annual Laurel Festival, which began in 1934, honoring the pale pink state flower that blooms abundantly in the area and its namesake. People come from around the country for the 3-day festival, which includes a parade, the crowning of a queen, and the Laurel Ball.

8.0   At the stop sign, proceed straight onto Rugg Brook Road, crossing Winchester Road (CT 263).

After a short, steep climb the road descends through the woods, with a particularly scenic stretch hugging the shores of Rugg Brook Reservoir and passing through Algonquin State Forest.

10.6   At the stop sign, turn left onto Norfolk Road (US 44).

11.5   Turn right onto Hannafin Road.

Continue straight as the road turns into Mill Brook Road.

13.0   At the stop sign, turn left onto Colebrook Road (CT 183).

Although this is a main avenue into Colebrook, it is a pleasant, mostly level road flanked by broad expanses of farmland.

14.2   In the village of Colebrook, turn right onto Smith Hill Road, between the Colebrook Congregational Church and the Colebrook Historical Society.

The charming yellow Greek Revival Colebrook Store has groceries and a deli. Inside, check out the original cast-iron woodstove in the back of the store.

Challenging terrain in the Litchfield Hills.

16.2 *At the stop sign, turn left onto Old North Road, then take an immediate left onto Deer Hill Road.*

Deer Hill Road makes a steep, winding descent; use caution.

17.7 *At the stop sign, turn left onto Colebrook River Road (US 8).*

19.3 *Turn left onto Sandy Brook Road.*

This quiet, narrow road winds through thick, shady Algonquin State Forest along boulder-strewn Sandy Brook.

23.2 *Turn right onto Phelps Flat Road.*

This turns into a short, well-maintained dirt road.

23.8 Turn right onto Colebrook Road (CT 183) to North Colebrook.

After riding through woods for several miles, the wide expanse of meadow along this part of the ride seems particularly striking.

24.3 At the tiny white North Colebrook Baptist Church, also known as Church in the Wildwood, turn left onto Church Hill Road.

This church was established in 1794; today it holds services from July to September. Church Hill Road is the first of several fairly strenuous climbs on the quiet forested roads that will take you through North Colebrook.

26.2 At the intersection of State Line Hill Road, bear left.

This road will turn into North Colebrook Road. You can glimpse Benedict Pond through the woods on the right.

26.8 Bear right onto Doolittle Drive.

You will see a sign for Doolittle Drive that indicates a left turn; instead, bear right.

27.9 Turn left, continuing on Doolittle Drive.

Wheeler Road goes to the right here.

28.8 After passing a large farm on the left, turn right onto Loon Meadow Drive.

This is a fast, fun descent past meadows and fine Colonial homes.

29.6 At the stop sign, turn left onto North Street (CT 272).

This road descends past Haystack Mountain State Park before climbing to the charming village of Norfolk. A 34-foot stone tower (1,716 feet) is perched atop 224 hilly acres and offers views of peaks in Massachusetts and New York. A road climbs halfway up the mountain; from there a rugged hiking trail leads to the tower.

31.1 At the stop sign, proceed straight onto CT 272/US 44.

31.4 At the Norfolk green, bear right onto Litchfield Road (CT 272).

33.2 Turn left onto Winchester Road at the sign for Winchester Lake.

This narrow country road winds for several miles, turning into

West Road at the Winchester town line before arriving at the green.

39.0 *At the stop sign, continue straight.*

39.5 *At the Winchester green, turn right onto Newfield Road.*

This is a long, gradual descent, an enjoyable way to end a long tour.

44.2 *Turn right into the parking area at the East Branch Dam, where the tour began.*

Bicycle Shops

Tommy's Bicycles & Fitness, 40 East Main Street (US 202), Torrington; 860-482-3571

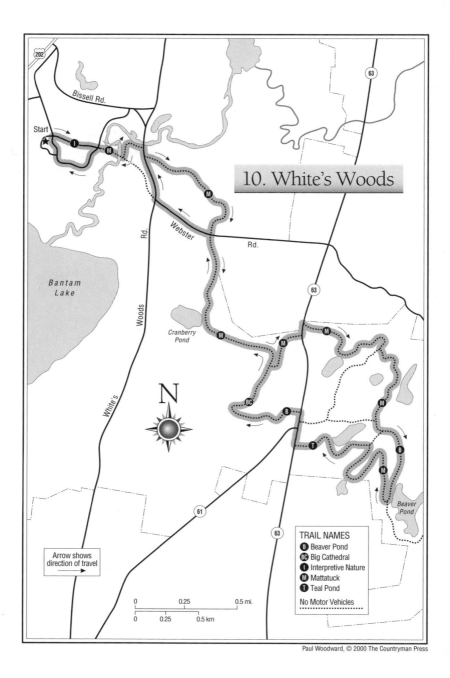

202

63

Bissell Rd.

Start

I

M

M

10. White's Woods

Webster

Rd.

Rd.

Bantam
Lake

Woods

63

Cranberry
Pond

M

M

M

Rd.

White's

N

BC

B

M

T

B

M

Beaver
Pond

61

63

Arrow shows
direction of travel

TRAIL NAMES
B Beaver Pond
BC Big Cathedral
I Interpretive Nature
M Mattatuck
T Teal Pond

No Motor Vehicles
·····················

0   0.25   0.5 mi.

0   0.25   0.5 km

10
White's Woods

Distance: *8.9 miles*
Terrain: *Easy dirt trails with some short climbs and descents*
Difficulty: *Moderate*
Recommended bicycle: *Mountain bike*

White Memorial Conservation Center and Museum is the state's largest nature center and wildlife sanctuary; 4,000 acres of woods, swamps, bogs, and meadows are blazed with an extensive 35-mile network of trails, some popular, others remote and solitary.

The natural beauty of this preserve is the legacy of Litchfield residents Alain C. White and his sister, May W. White. In 1908 they bequested their land around Bantam Lake (the largest natural lake in Connecticut) and the surrounding woods and countryside to ensure its preservation.

The result of their tremendous foresight and love of nature is the home of a diverse natural population of birds and animals. Open fields are good for spotting deer, cottontail rabbits, and wild turkeys. The marsh areas are prime natural habitats for great blue herons, beavers, mallards, wood ducks, red-winged blackbirds, and many other birds—nearly 250 species have been reported in the sanctuary. More than 165 varieties of wildflowers grow in the gently sloping meadows and cool forests of oak, white pine, and hemlock. When riding through the forest, it's not uncommon to hear the echoing hoots of owls and the hammering of woodpeckers, especially in the early morning and evening hours.

Most of the ride follows rolling doubletrack trails through a variety of habitats, from marsh to pine forest. The hills are moderate to steep but short, with occasional areas of loose rock or other minor obstructions. There are many other trails and dirt roads in addition to what is described here. Some trails are open only to hikers; please respect trail closures. The information booth at the start of the ride has a detailed map of the preserve; maps are also posted at each trailhead and are sold in the museum gift shop.

The grounds at White Memorial are a picnicker's paradise; food and supplies can be found in either direction on US 202, in Bantam to the west or east toward Litchfield. The recently renovated museum (860-567-0857) features excellent exhibits on Connecticut's natural history and the local wildlife a visitor might observe on the grounds at different seasons of the year. It also has a comprehensive nature library.

Directions for the Ride

From US 202, south of the Litchfield green, turn left onto Bissell Road and then take an immediate right onto unpaved Whitehall Road. Look for the large brown White Memorial Conservation Center sign, which can be seen from US 202. About 0.5 mile down the entrance road you'll arrive at a cluster of buildings; park in the lot next to the information kiosk.

0.0 *From the parking lot, head down the dirt road that passes in front of the museum.*

The road descends gently past a field lined with large sugar maples and white pines before entering the woods.

0.2 *Go straight at the T-intersection, passing through a wrought-iron fence with stone gateposts.*

Follow this flat path to a wood-plank bridge above the Bantam River. Make an immediate left after crossing the bridge, so the river is on the left of the trail and a paddock is to your right. Pass through a rock barrier and enter a small parking lot and boat-launch area.

0.5 *Turn right onto Whites Woods Road (unmarked) for about 50 yards, then turn left into the woods at the first trailhead.*

Look for the telltale brown gate and map that designate most trail-heads in the preserve. This flat, scenic trail is clearly marked with blue blazes on trees. Watch for equestrians and hikers in this popular area.

1.0 At the Y-intersection, follow the blue trail to the right.

Here the trail leads into Catlin Woods. Watch out for soft sand hidden under the blanket of pine needles covering this trail.

1.3 At the trailhead, cross Webster Road (an unmarked dirt road).

The woods open onto Cranberry Swamp on this long, flat stretch of the blue trail.

2.3 At the fork, follow the blue trail to the left (look for blue arrow on a tree).

Gradually descend to another trailhead.

2.5 Pass through the gate and turn left on South Plains Road (CT 63). Go about 20 yards, then turn right into the woods at another trailhead.

2.9 At the intersection, follow the blue blazes to the left.

A short detour to the right here will take you to Heron Pond. You'll start a winding, moderate climb here.

3.2 Follow the blue arrow to the left at the fork (the red-blazed trail goes right).

Continue climbing for a short distance, then begin winding downhill; watch for rocks, roots, and other minor obstructions. At a row of stone posts you'll pass high above the Plunge Pool. From here, the trail flattens and becomes doubletrack with a grassy median.

3.8 At a Y-intersection, turn left onto a trail blazed with both blue and white.

Stay on this fast downhill trail until you reach Beaver Pond on the left.

4.4 At Beaver Pond, turn right onto the blue trail and immediately begin a steep climb.

This loose, rocky trail improves when it flattens and winds around the top.

5.2 At the Y-intersection, turn left (the blue trail goes straight here).

This little-used doubletrack section becomes grassy and overgrown and passes Teal Pond and two narrow, orange-blazed trails near its shore.

5.6 *At the trailhead, turn right onto Litchfield Road (CT 63) for about 200 yards, pass the junction of CT 61, then turn left into the woods at the first trailhead.*

This trailhead is shrouded by trees and difficult to spot, so look closely for the map and gate. There is also a green sign for the towns of Morris, Bethlehem, and Watertown near the trailhead. Begin a fun downhill on this trail.

6.3 *At a five-way trail intersection, take a hard right onto the orange-blazed trail.*

You'll follow the orange blazes for a short time; when they turn right up a narrow steep trail, continue straight on the unmarked doubletrack trail.

6.6 *Immediately continue straight to connect to the blue trail; do not turn right here.*

Pass through Cranberry Swamp again. After a short climb, bear left at the fork.

7.6 *Pass through the trailhead gate, then turn left onto Webster Road (unmarked).*

8.0 *At the stop sign, turn right onto Whites Woods Road. Just before the bridge, turn left into the boat-launch area and reenter the woods through the row of boulders. Follow the trail along the Bantam River and bear right onto the wooden bridge.*

8.5 *Pass through the stone gateposts and turn left onto the dirt park road.*

This road will take you out of the woods, through a meadow, and back to the parking lot, where the ride ends. Ongley Pond is a good spot for an end-of-ride picnic; wooden tables are along the water's edge and in the meadow next to the museum.

Bicycle Shops

Cycle Loft, 25 Commons Drive (US 202), Litchfield; 860-567-1713

11
Gaylordsville to Sherman

Distance: 16.8 miles, with two short side trips
Terrain: Rolling hills with a few moderately steep climbs; two dirt roads
Difficulty: Moderate
Recommended bicycle: Touring/road bike

Gaylordsville was a dairy- and tobacco-farming community when it was settled in northwest New Milford in 1725. Today it still retains its agricultural character although only a handful of farms remain.

The Gaylord School, built in 1740, was the last one-room schoolhouse that operated in Connecticut. In 1760 the town began collecting taxes to fund the school and pay the teacher's salary, which by 1849 had risen to $1.25 a week. Many of the students walked from nearby farms to attend classes in the tiny school, which was kept warm by a pot-belly stove. The school didn't switch over to electric lights and oil heat until 1935; before that it was still lit with kerosene lamps and heated with wood or coal. Running water and toilets finally arrived in the 1950s. The school closed its doors in 1967 after educating students for 227 years.

You'll pass Colonial saltboxes weathered into faded earth colors along the back roads to Sherman, Gaylordsville's quiet neighbor to the south. The quaint village looks much as it did when it was founded in 1802 and named for Roger Sherman, the only American to sign the Declaration of Independence, the Articles of Association, the Articles of Confederation, and the federal Constitution.

Back in Gaylordsville, a short side trip will take you to the restored 1843 Merwinsville Hotel, the only railroad hotel east of the Mississippi River and one of the oldest in the country. Gaylordsville resident Sylvanus Merwin learned in 1842 that a new railroad line would be built through

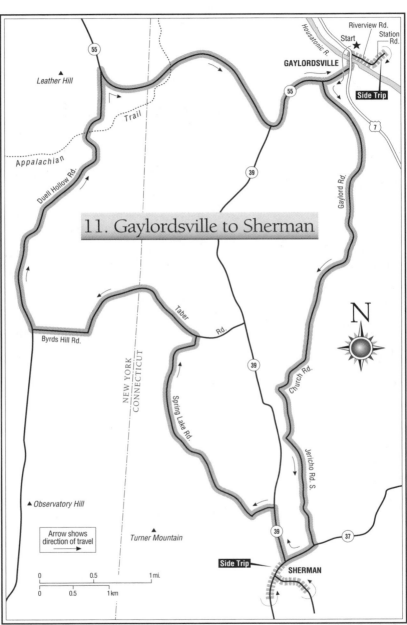

Riverview Rd.
Station
Rd.
Start
GAYLORDSVILLE
Housatonic R.
55
55
Leather Hill
Trail
Appalachian
Duell Hollow Rd.
39
Side Trip
7
Gaylord Rd

11. Gaylordsville to Sherman

N

Byrds Hill Rd.
Taber
Rd.
39
NEW YORK
CONNECTICUT
Spring Lake Rd.
Church Rd.
Jericho Rd. S.

Observatory Hill

Arrow shows
direction of travel

Turner Mountain

39

37

Side Trip
SHERMAN

0   0.5   1 mi.
0   0.5   1 km

Paul Woodward, © 2000 The Countryman Press

town. He found out exactly where the route would pass, purchased some land on the east bank of the Housatonic River, and put up a hotel. When officials from the Housatonic Line came to Merwin seeking a right-of-way through his property, he demanded that the hotel be a meal stop and that the station be named for him.

The three-story hotel opened on Browns Forge Road in 1843 and served the town and the rail line for 50 years. Steam engines pulled coaches full of businessmen, soldiers, and wealthy vacationers from Long Island Sound to the Berkshire Hills, stopping first at the Merwinsville Station for lunch before continuing north along the Housatonic River. The elegant hotel had a ballroom, wine cellar, and ticket office; Merwin was the ticket agent.

The hotel served meals here until 1877, when the advent of the Pullman dining car and faster trains made luncheon stops unnecessary. The ticket office remained open until 1915.

A 1970s restoration put the hotel on the National Register of Historic Places. It's open for free tours on Sunday from July through September; call 860-350-4443.

Directions for the Ride

Begin at the pale yellow Gaylordsville Country Store just off US 7 in the village of Gaylordsville. You can also park along Riverview Road.

0.0 *Turn left onto Kent Road (US 7), cross the Housatonic River, and take the first right onto Webatuck Road (CT 55).*

0.4 *Take the first left onto Newton Road East, keeping left at the T-intersection.*

This dirt road will turn to pavement in 0.5 mile. You'll ride past the red barns of Newton Farm, established in 1894.

0.8 *Turn right onto Gaylord Road.*

Across the intersection is the Washington Oak; look for a white sign hanging from the trunk of this massive tree, estimated to be 400 years old. In September 1780, Gen. George Washington met here with the Marquis de Lafayette and other members of his staff to eat a noon meal before continuing on their journey to meet with Count de Rochambeau in Hartford.

About 0.5 mile from the oak tree you'll see the tiny red Gaylord School with its neat white shutters. The school is open to visitors 2–5 PM Sunday in July and August.

You'll ride past some fine old Colonial homes before reaching a tiny cemetery behind a wrought-iron gate. William Gaylord and his wife, who moved here in 1712 from New Milford, were the first to be buried here. Among the timeworn headstones are the graves of several Revolutionary War soldiers.

2.3 Bear right onto Church Road (Stilson Hill Road is to the left).

Cross into the town of Sherman just after this intersection. After about 2 miles you'll pass the lovely 1892 Sherman Congregational Church.

4.3 Turn left onto Jericho Road North.

This will turn to dirt, climb through the woods, and narrow into a rough dirt path that connects to Jericho Road South on the other side.

5.4 At the traffic light, turn right onto East Sherman Road (CT 37). Descend south toward the village of Sherman.

5.7 At the traffic light, turn right onto CT 39.

Side Trip: Continue straight on CT 37 to see the lovely colonial village of Sherman—its white clapboard buildings, tiny brick Sherman Library, historical society museum, and the Old Store, circa 1810. A wooden sign at Saw Mill Road designates the center of this quaint 200-year-old town. The iron carving atop the sign, of a farmer plowing with a team of oxen, is a nod to the town's agricultural roots. There is a pizza restaurant and gift shop on Saw Mill Road.

6.3 Turn left onto Spring Lake Road.

The road will climb slowly into the woods before opening to rolling meadows lined with gnarled old oaks and stone walls.

8.7 At the stop sign, turn left onto Taber Road.

9.2 At the stop sign, bear left at the Y-intersection.

This quiet rural road leads to the New York border.

10.6 Make a sharp right turn onto Byrds Hill Road.

The 1740 Gaylord School was the last operating one-room schoolhouse in Connecticut.

After about 0.5 mile, the road turns to dirt; take this steep, winding descent slowly.

11.9 *At the stop sign (remnants of a stone chimney are straight ahead), turn right onto Duell Hollow Road.*

A short, steep climb gives way to a long descent past Camp Siwanoy (a scout reservation and wildlife preserve) and the Appalachian Trail, on its well-worn 2,100-mile course from Springer Mountain, Georgia, to Mount Katahdin in Maine.

13.5 *Turn right onto US 55.*

This road crosses back into New Milford.

16.7 *At the stop sign, turn left onto Kent Road (US 7).*

16.8 *The tour ends at the Gaylordsville Country Store across the bridge.*

Side Trip: To get to the Merwinsville Hotel from the Gaylordsville Country Store, turn left onto Riverview Road, past the Village Café. About 0.25 mile down the road, bear left at the red barn onto Station Road. Climb a short hill to the railroad tracks, then bear left onto Brown's Forge Road. You'll see the rambling white clapboard hotel on the left next to the tracks.

Bicycle Shops

Bicycle Center, 612 Federal Road (US 7 and US 202), Brookfield; 203-775-7083

Bike Express, 73 Bridge Street (CT 67 and US 202), New Milford; 860-354-1466

NORTH
COUNTRY

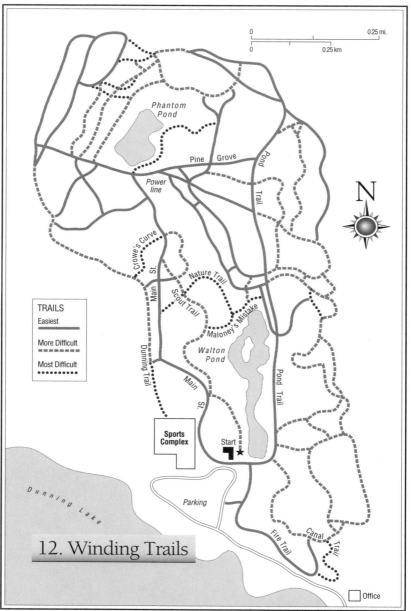

0.25 mi.

0.25 km

Phantom
Pond

Pine Grove

Power
line

Pond

Trail

N

Crowe's Curve

Main St.

Nature Trail

Scout Trail

Maloney's Mistake

TRAILS
Easiest
More Difficult
Most Difficult

Dunning Trail

Walton
Pond

Main St.

Pond Trail

Sports
Complex

Start
★

Dunning Lake

Parking

Fire Trail

Canal Trail

12. Winding Trails

Office

Paul Woodward, © 2000 The Countryman Press

12
Winding Trails

Distance: *12 miles of trails*
Terrain: *Flat and moderately rolling cross-country ski trails*
Difficulty: *Easy*
Recommended bicycle: *Mountain bike*

Winter-sports enthusiasts have been coming to Winding Trails since 1975 to ski its extensive network of cross-country trails. In recent years, this private facility in Farmington has followed the lead of many New England ski areas by opening its snow-free trails to mountain bikers during the off-season.

The Winding Trails Cross Country Ski & Mountain Bike Center (860-678-9582) is one of the most user-friendly, well-maintained, and clearly marked mountain biking areas in the state. The scenic 12-mile network of blissfully solitary trails will make an excellent day of mountain biking for riders of all abilities. Beginners will love it here because it's nearly impossible to get lost or end up on a trail that is too difficult. Each trail junction—and there are many—is clearly marked with the trail name and its level of difficulty. The wooded trails are also ideal for people riding with children; the network is so tightly interconnected that it's easy to return to the trailhead quickly if you want to end the ride early or just need to fill water bottles or use the bathroom.

The flip side for some mountain bikers may be the lack of adventure, if that's what you're looking for. No trail on this 350-acre woodland tract is unmarked or undiscovered, and overall the terrain is easy to moderate—some of the trails rated most difficult can probably be handled by a skilled beginner. And unlike state parks and private land trusts, cyclists are charged a $5 trail fee to ride here. Dogs are not allowed on the trails.

Cruising along a ski trail in Farmington.

However, those looking for a challenge should keep in mind that the Winding Trails Fat Tire Classic is the opening race in the National Off Road Mountain Biking Association (NORBA) Connecticut Point Series. The Winding Trails race takes place each spring; for information, contact local bike shops.

Directions for the Ride

From I-84, take exit 39 and follow Farmington Avenue (CT 4) west into Farmington. Cross the bridge over the Farmington River and turn right at the second traffic light onto Devonwood Drive. Take the first left onto Winding Trails Drive and stop at the gatehouse to pick up a trail map. Follow the road to its end and park in one of the lots around the sports complex.

Winding Trails offers such a plethora of beautiful trails—you can spend hours connecting endless combinations of them—that highlighting one ride would be a disservice. Half the fun here is planning your own route or having the freedom to make random decisions at each junction. Be sure to carry a trail map with you to orient yourself when it's time to head back to the trailhead. You can pick up the trails behind the ski lodge; follow the hill toward Walton Pond and ride across the small beach to Pond Trail.

A roughly 2-mile loop of easy trails that makes an ideal warm-up is to take the wide, flat Pond Trail north into the woods, following the east shore of Walton Pond. At a Y-intersection, turn left onto Pine Grove, then turn left again to join the trail that parallels a power line. Turn back into the woods onto Main Street (a wide dirt road) to return to the trailhead.

A longer, more challenging circuit with many short, steep climbs begins at Pond Trail and turns right onto Fire Trail, which leads straight onto Canal Trail. Bear right when Canal Trail splits, following your choice of blue-blazed intermediate trails along the eastern edge of the park. Cut back across Pond Trail at the northern tip of Walton Pond to Nature's Trail and Maloney's Mistake; turn right on Scout Trail to Crowe's Curve; and make a final left turn onto Dunning Trail, following it back to the sports complex.

Bicycle Shops

Central Wheel, 62 Farmington Avenue (CT 4), Farmington; 860-677-7010

Farmington Bicycle Shop, 222 Main Street (CT 10), Farmington; 860-677-2453

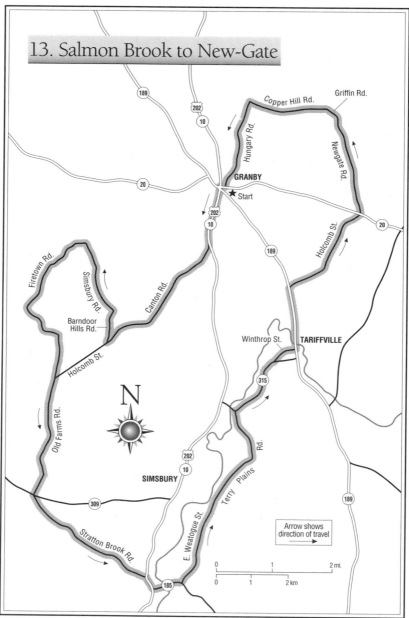

13. Salmon Brook to New-Gate

189

202

10

189

202

10

20

Copper Hill Rd.

Griffin Rd.

Hungary Rd.

Newgate Rd.

GRANBY

★ Start

20

189

Holcomb St.

Firetown Rd.

Simsbury Rd.

Canton Rd.

Barndoor
Hills Rd.

Holcomb St.

Winthrop St.

TARIFFVILLE

315

Old Farms Rd.

N

202

10

SIMSBURY

Terry Plains Rd.

189

Arrow shows
direction of travel

309

E. Weatogue St.

Stratton Brook Rd.

185

0   1   2 mi.

0   1   2 km

Paul Woodward, © 2000 The Countryman Press

13

Salmon Brook to New-Gate

Distance: *28.5 miles*
Terrain: *Rolling hills with flat sections along the Farmington River*
Difficulty: *Moderate*
Recommended bicycle: *Touring/road bike*

Along many of these wooded back roads you will ride past evidence of Hartford's sprawl, which has created a patchwork of farm, forest, and quiet suburb with historic enclaves in between.

A cluster of well-preserved buildings in Granby is all that remains of the Salmon Brook settlement, a former village built in the 18th century. In 1858 East Granby was known as the Turkey Hills Ecclesiastical Society, which was a settlement of only a handful of families until copper deposits were discovered on a nearby hillside.

A group of land proprieters from Simsbury formed a company to mine the hills, despite the fact that the mining and smelting of copper was in defiance of British law. North America's first chartered copper mine opened in 1707, from which the colonies' first copper coins were produced and stamped "I am good Copper."

When copper ceased to be profitable, the mine was converted into the colonial government's first prison during the American Revolution. Robbers, counterfeiters, and horse thieves along with Tories and war criminals languished in the subterranean tunnels and dark recesses of the mine, some 70 feet below ground. The prison was called New-Gate, named for one of England's most wretched prisons.

Old New-Gate Prison and Copper Mine (860-653-3563) is open to the public; if you choose not to tour the mine's damp underground passageways, you can enjoy the lovely picnic grounds with sweeping views of the surrounding countryside and the Berkshire Hills to the north.

The ride also takes you across the Farmington River on an iron bridge. On the opposite bank is the gargantuan Pinchot Sycamore, the state's largest tree. Here along the banks of the river are traces of the region's colonial history, preserved in two quiet historic districts and the working farms that surround them.

Directions for the Ride

The ride begins at Valley Bicycle in the Granby Village Shops on Hartford Avenue (CT 189).

0.0 *From the parking lot, turn right onto Hartford Avenue (CT 189).*

0.1 *At the traffic light, turn left onto Salmon Brook Street (US 202/CT 10).*

You will pass some of Granby's oldest homes, pretty Colonials and Victorians on wide, leafy lawns. Just down the road on the left are the meticulously restored colonial-era buildings maintained by the Salmon Brook Historical Society. The church society of Salmon Brook, settled in the early 1700s, became incorporated as the farming town of Granby in 1786.

The remains of this early settlement include a white one-room schoolhouse, c. 1865, and two 18th-century clapboard homes: the Weed-Enders House and the Abijah Rowe House, a saltbox built by the farmer and blacksmith when he moved to the settlement in 1753. Also on site is a tobacco barn built in the early 20th century. The large barn is now a museum (860-653-9713) exhibiting artifacts of early agriculture and industry as well as Civil War and Native American history.

1.2 *Shortly after you pass the McLean Game Refuge, turn right onto Canton Road.*

This 3,400-acre preserve left by early 20th-century governor George McLean offers picnicking, birding, and hiking in the Barn-door Hills. This lovely woodland tract was set aside to protect native trees, flowers, and wildlife, including deer, fox, coyote, bear, and migrating geese during the spring and fall. The next few miles are shaded by the preserve's towering pines.

3.1 *At the stop sign, continue straight on Holcomb Street.*

America's first copper mine, opened in 1707, later became New-Gate prison.

3.8 *Turn right at this stop sign onto Barndoor Hills Road.*

4.4 *At the stop sign, turn left onto Simsbury Road.*

You'll tackle a moderately steep 0.5-mile climb before plunging down the other side.

5.8 *Turn left onto Firetown Road.*

This especially scenic stretch winds through the woods at the base of the West Mountains.

8.4 *Turn right onto Old Farms Road.*

9.2 *Go straight at the stop sign.*

The woods turn into open meadows with rural views, restored antique homes, and a produce farm scattered among the newer houses.

11.4 *At the traffic light, go straight onto Stratton Brook Road.*

This section of leafy suburbs becomes flat and winding.

12.8 *At the next traffic light, continue straight.*

In the Weatogue section of Simsbury, turn right onto busy US 202 for a short time, taking the first left onto CT 185.

Here you'll pass over the Farmington River on an iron bridge. Just after the traffic light at the bridge's far end, you'll see massive gnarled branches stretching 93 feet into the air. Turn into the gated dirt trailhead on the left to get a closer look at the Gifford Pinchot Sycamore, Connecticut's largest tree. The impossibly huge trunk has a circumference of 25 feet, 8 inches. The tiny 3-acre park here on the bank of the Farmington River makes a good lunch stop; supplies can be picked up along US 202.

14.8 Turn left onto East Weatogue Street.

Use caution at this rotarylike intersection, which leads to the East Weatogue Historic District, one of Simsbury's earliest farming settlements, where cornfields still stretch along the Farmington River. You can enjoy the bounty by stopping at one of several roadside produce stands. A Massacoh Indian village site in this area of Colonial and Greek Revival farmhouses has produced many artifacts dating back 8,000 years.

16.4 At the stop sign, bear right onto Terry's Plain Road.

The flat, open fields in the Terry's Plain Historic District make for pleasant, effortless riding. The broad, fertile plain is flanked on the west by the Farmington River and on the east by the Metacomet Ridge. It has been farmed since 1653, when pine trees were harvested for the shipbuilding industry; tobacco was a cash crop during the Civil War. It was also the site of the first ferry on the Farmington River and training grounds for the Simsbury militia. The plain hasn't changed much in the past 350 years, and working farms and acres of crops still blanket the flat expanse.

17.7 Bear left at the stop sign.

18.5 At this stop sign, turn right onto Tariffville Road (CT 315).

19.6 Turn left onto Winthrop Street and descend into the village of Tariffville.

This historic mill village on the Farmington River isn't a tourist destination, which makes it all the more authentic and charming. The mills were powered by water from a nearby gorge in the Farmington River, and an 1824 tariff imposed on imported goods made wool cloth and carpet manufacturing very marketable. Scottish weavers were brought here in the early 19th century to work in the mills of the Tariffville Manufacturing Company. The mill housing has been preserved, along with the Greek and Gothic Revival buildings that came in the late 1800s. Nearly 200 buildings in this small village are on the National Register of Historic Places.

19.9 *In the center of Tariffville, turn right onto Main Street, then almost immediately bear left onto Hartford Avenue (CT 189).*

21.0 *At the traffic light, turn right onto Holcomb Road.*

23.1 *Go straight onto New-Gate Road.*

Near the crest of Peak Mountain you'll see the crumbling walls of Old New-Gate prison. It cost the colonial government $375 to purchase and convert the copper mine into a prison. Across the street is the historic Viets Tavern, an 18th-century center-chimney Colonial where several generations of the Viet family lived for nearly 200 years. Capt. John Viet's wife ran the tavern, which offered "bed, board & grog," first to miners, then later to people visiting prisoners. Abraham Lincoln stayed in an upstairs bedroom in 1860 on his way to Boston.

A turn-of-the-20th-century tavern menu in the New-Gate visitors center features Old New England lager and ice cream for a dime, an omelet with french fries for 45 cents, and broiled chicken with fries and vegetables for 65 cents.

24.9 *At the stop sign, turn left onto Copper Hill Road; continue on it as it forks left at the golf course.*

This flat ribbon of road passes along a peaceful community of working farms.

26.5 *Turn left onto Hungary Road.*

28.2 *At the stop sign, turn right onto CT 20/CT 189.*

28.3 *At the traffic light, turn left.*

28.4 *At the next light, make another left.*

28.5 *Turn left into the Granby Village Shops to end the ride.*

Bicycle Shops

The Bicycle Cellar, 532 Hopmeadow Street, Simsbury; 860-658-1311

Valley Bicycle & Repair Shop, Inc., 10 Hartford Avenue (CT 189), Granby; 860-653-6545

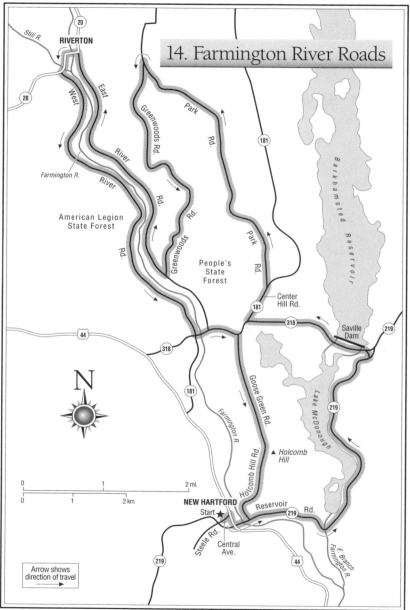

14. Farmington River Roads

Still R.

RIVERTON

20

20

West

East

Greenwoods Rd.

Park

Rd.

181

River

River

Farmington R.

River

Rd.

American Legion
State Forest

Greenwoods

Rd.

Rd.

Greenwoods

Rd.

People's
State
Forest

Park

Rd.

Barkhamsted Reservoir

Center
Hill Rd.

181

318

Saville
Dam

219

44

318

181

Goose Green Rd.

Farmington R.

Lake McDonough

219

219

N

Holcomb Hill Rd.

▲ Holcomb
Hill

0   1   2 mi.

0   1   2 km

NEW HARTFORD
Start ★

Reservoir   Rd.

219

Steele Rd.

Central
Ave.

219

44

E. Branch
Farmington R.

Arrow shows
direction of travel
———▶

14
Farmington River Roads

Distance: *25.2 miles*
Terrain: *Winding and hilly roads, except for those along the Farmington River*
Difficulty: *Moderate to strenuous*
Recommended bicycle: *Touring/road bike*

This scenic ride takes you deep into the rugged forests of north-central Connecticut, a pristine area that hasn't changed much since the 19th century, thanks to the presence of two state forests—People's and American Legion—as well as Metropolitan District Commission property surrounding the Barkhamsted Reservoir and Lake McDonough.

People's State Forest has many excellent picnicking spots and secluded hiking trails, each named for the people—Henry Buck, Jessie Girard, Agnes Bowen, and Elliott Bronson, among others—who helped preserve this cool, dense forest. Along the yellow-blazed Jessie Girard trail is the site of the famed Barkhamsted Lighthouse. According to lore, a local settler's daughter married a Native American (against her father's wishes) and moved to a Native American settlement in the rugged hills. A light shining from their cabin window was a beacon for stagecoach drivers, who then knew they were only a few miles from New Hartford. Many artifacts from Native American campsites have been discovered throughout the forest. Another hiking trail leads to a soapstone quarry on a ledge outcrop high in the forest that was worked by Native Americans 4,000 years ago.

The narrow forest road through People's is a roller-coaster ride: a long, slow climb and a fast, winding descent down the other side, complete with sharp turns. Near the bottom is a rustic stone building, built by the Civilian Conservation Corps in 1934, which houses the forest office and a small museum (860-379-6118) featuring interpretive programs that highlight the area's natural history and environment.

East and West River Roads flank the Farmington River, a stretch of water popular with local fly-fishermen. The river is right beside you as you pedal these country lanes punctuated with secluded picnic spots. The stretch of river between Riverton and New Hartford has been designated a Wild and Scenic River, one of only four in New England.

In the heart of this area lies Riverton, a serene little hamlet that seems frozen in time. The nerve center of this 18th-century river town is the Riverton General Store, where you can buy groceries and read the results of local fishing derbies posted on the porch. The Hitchcock Factory, a colossal 18th-century factory on the banks of the Farmington River, still produces its signature hand-stenciled furniture. Connecticut's smallest country fair is held here each October, marking the end of the fair season.

This tour begins in the Victorian village of New Hartford, which sits at the junction of Main Street (US 44) and Reservoir Road (CT 219), on the west branch of the Farmington River. New Hartford was settled in 1733 when this wooded area of the state was called "the Greenwoods." Chatterly's, at Two Bridge Street, is a Victorian gem serving lunch and dinner in the former New Hartford Hotel, a village landmark.

Directions for the Ride

Park in the commuter lot on Church Street North, behind the white Immaculate Conception Church on Main Street.

0.0 *From the parking lot, turn left onto Central Avenue, passing the white-columned New Hartford Memorial Library and the tiny, brown-shingled town hall.*

0.1 *At the traffic light, turn right onto Main Street (US 44).*

0.2 *At this traffic light, turn left onto Reservoir Road (CT 219).*

Cross the west branch of the Farmington River and head north, climbing gradually into the woods toward Lake McDonough. Here the road flattens; hugs the east shore of this long, evergreen-lined lake; and crosses into Barkhamsted.

4.0 *Bear left onto Saville Dam Road (CT 318) and cross over Saville Dam on the Barkhamsted Reservoir.*

A stone gatehouse standing sentinel over the Barkhamsted Reservoir.

Pass by stone walls and ride by this scenic reservoir and the c. 1940 stone gatehouse with its massive wooden door. This road over the dam can get busy (it's a popular back-road route to Bradley International Airport), so use caution.

When you leave the reservoir, a short climb leads to a plunging descent that should provide enough momentum to bring you almost to the top of the next climb.

5.6 Turn right onto Center Hill Road (CT 181).

This road heads north toward People's State Forest. At the crest of a short, steep climb, look for a brown tree farm sign on the left; this will be your next turn.

6.1 Turn left onto Park Road.

This cool, shaded, quiet road climbs a steep hill that mellows at the top into rolling hills, passing only a few old houses before rising again.

9.7 Turn left onto Greenwoods Road (unmarked), a gated road that leads into People's State Forest.

Use caution while negotiating the rough surface of this steep road; don't build up too much speed.

13.2 Turn right onto East River Road.

The west branch of the Farmington River will be on your left; you can picnic or just rest in the shade of 200-year-old pines growing along the riverbank in Mathies Grove.

15.7 Turn left onto Riverton Road (CT 20) into the tiny village of Riverton.

The Hitchcock Museum in the Old Union Church features 18th-
and 19th-century ornamented Hitchcock furniture and related memorabilia; it's open by appointment only. Call the Riverton Factory Store at 860-379-4826.

The Riverton General Store has a deli and is open daily 6 AM–7 PM. Across the street, the Village Sweet Shoppe has great ice cream. The neat 1880 yellow Victorian in town is a small restaurant (860-379-7020) aptly named the Yellow Victorian, offering eclectic American cuisine and a Sunday brunch.

15.9 Cross the Farmington River and immediately turn left onto West River Road.

This follows the river south into the Pleasant Valley section of Barkhamsted.

20.1 At the stop sign, turn left onto the steel bridge crossing the river (CT 318/181).

Begin a steep, 0.5-mile climb away from the river.

20.6 At the crest of the hill, turn right onto Goose Green Road.

This turns into Holcomb Hill Road as you cross into New Hartford.

22.7 At the next two stop signs, continue straight.

23.1 Turn right onto Reservoir Road (CT 219) and cross the Farmington River.

25.0 At the traffic light, turn right onto Main Street (US 44) in New Hartford.

25.1 At the next light, turn left onto Central Avenue.

Follow this short street to the commuter parking lot to end the ride.

Bicycle Shops

Benidorm Bikes & Boards, 247 Albany Turnpike (US 44), Canton; 860-693-8891

Country Sports, 65 Albany Turnpike (US 44), Canton; 860-693-0266

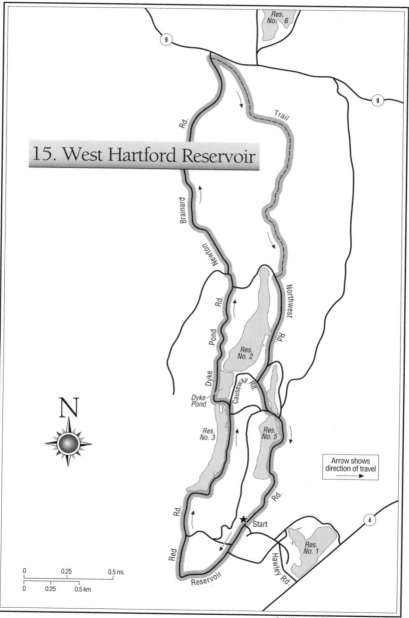

15. West Hartford Reservoir

Res. No. 6

9

9

Trail

Rd.

Brainard

Newton

Northwest Rd.

Rd.

Pond

Dyke

Res. No. 2

Dyke Pond

Causeway Rd.

Res. No. 3

Res. No. 5

Arrow shows
direction of travel

N

Rd.

★ Start

Red

Rd.

Res. No. 1

4

Hawley Rd.

Reservoir

0   0.25   0.5 mi.
0   0.25   0.5 km

Paul Woodward, © 2000 The Countryman Press

15
West Hartford Reservoir

Distance: *8.2 miles*
Terrain: *Dirt roads and doubletrack dirt trails; one paved bike lane*
Difficulty: *Moderate*
Recommended bicycle: *Mountain bike*

The Metropolitan District Commission's (MDC's) Talcott Mountain Reservoir area is one of the state's premier mountain biking locations, and a few years ago cyclists almost lost it for good.

In 1997, MDC officials had considered banning mountain biking and other "high-risk" recreation from reservoir lands. First it was because of conflicts between various users of the park; later on it became an issue of liability. An agreement was reached between the MDC and local mountain bikers, who created a volunteer bike-patrol network to promote safety on the trails and in turn preserve public access to this beautiful piece of land.

Five reservoirs and 3,000 acres of woodland—incredibly scenic and secluded considering downtown Hartford is only minutes away—run along the base of Talcott Mountain. The Metacomet Trail, part of the state system of blue-blazed trails, passes through the park and joins this loop for a short time. The ride begins near the MDC water treatment plant in West Hartford and follows the base of Talcott Mountain to US 44. You return by riding across a series of dikes surrounded by expansive meadows, then back into the forest.

This is a popular spot for picnickers, walkers, in-line skaters, and cyclists; however, most park users stay on the paved bike paths, so once you venture onto the dirt roads and trails, you'll run into few people. Use caution when riding on the bike paths; let people know of your presence when approaching them from behind.

Members of the volunteer Mountain Bike Patrol Team, run by the

Connecticut chapter of the New England Mountain Biking Association (NEMBA), wear red jerseys and can assist with directions or minor mechanical problems. These patrollers are also first aid and CPR certified and carry cellular phones to report emergencies. The MDC requires all cyclists to wear helmets when riding on reservoir property.

This loop is but a small taste of what this extensive trail system has to offer; in all there are more than 30 miles of wooded roads and trails. For more challenging riding, try some of the trails that go up onto Talcott Mountain, but respect marked trail closures. Large, detailed maps of the reservoir area are posted at various spots along the trails and parking areas. Maps can also be purchased in the administration office near the entrance or by calling 860-278-7850. The trails are open daily from dawn to dusk.

Directions for the Ride

The entrance to Talcott Mountain Reservoir is on the north side of Farmington Avenue (CT 4) in West Hartford near the Farmington town line, about 1.5 miles west of West Hartford Center. Look for a traffic light and a sign for the MDC water treatment plant. Drive to the back parking lot, following signs along the park road for the bike paths.

0.0 *From the parking lot, turn right onto the paved one-way bike path.*

Cyclists must ride single file on this bike lane.

0.5 *Follow the paved bike path as it curves right, climbs into the woods, and flattens at the top.*

This is a diverse forest of oak, hickory, maple, birch, and elm. Climb another short rise, then follow the path to the right (a dirt trail goes left) past Reservoir #3. This scenic, twisty stretch hugs the rocky shoreline.

1.8 *Take the first left past the reservoir onto a wide dirt bike path, skirting the reservoir on one side and Dyke Pond on the other.*

The path rises into the woods and above the pond for a short time before turning deeper into the Newton Brainard Forest. The rolling terrain linked with flat stretches is shrouded by an almost continuous canopy of trees.

2.7 *At the Y-intersection, bear left. You'll shortly arrive at a similar junction, where you'll go right. At the third Y-intersection, bear left.*

3.5 *The trail emerges from the woods at power lines; bear right and eventually descend back into the trees on rough, loose pavement. Halfway down, bear left (a dirt road goes to the right).*
The road returns to hard-packed dirt and cuts through grassy fields enveloped by woods.

4.5 *Just before the gate that separates the trail from Albany Avenue (US 44), turn right onto a narrow gravel path.*
Here you'll ride over the Talcott Reservoir Flood Control Dike, a quiet area of beautiful open fields of tall grass and marshes dotted with trees.

5.1 *At the Y-intersection, turn right onto a narrow gravel path that skirts a meadow. At the next Y, turn right into the woods. When you emerge into more fields, bear right at the Y, up a short incline, then straight across a four-way intersection of single-track (the woods will be on your left). At the bottom of a short hill, bear left into the woods onto a wide, hard-packed dirt trail.*

6.1 *Bear right as the trail forks here.*

6.3 *Turn left onto this dirt park road.*

6.6 *Turn right onto the paved bike path and then immediately left onto a dirt trail in the woods, just before the paved path ascends a hill.*

6.7 *Turn left onto the paved bike path.*

7.0 *Turn left onto another paved bike path and follow the painted bike lane for about 1 mile along Reservoir #5 to the parking lot.*
There are several inviting picnic spots along the reservoir.

8.2 *Turn right into the parking lot to end the ride.*

Bicycle Shops

Central Wheel, 62 Farmington Avenue (CT 4), Farmington; 860-677-7010

THE QUIET CORNER

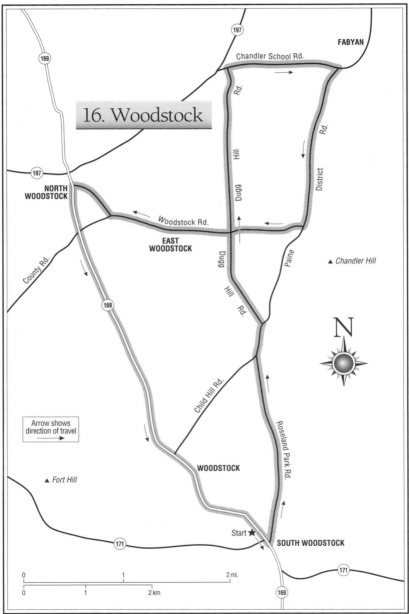

16. Woodstock

169

197

FABYAN

Chandler School Rd.

Hill Rd.

District Rd.

Dugg

197

NORTH WOODSTOCK

Woodstock Rd.

EAST WOODSTOCK

Dugg

Paine

▲ *Chandler Hill*

County Rd.

Hill Rd.

N

169

Child Hill Rd.

Arrow shows direction of travel

Roseland Park Rd.

WOODSTOCK

▲ Fort Hill

Start ★

SOUTH WOODSTOCK

171

169

| 0 | | 1 | | 2 mi. |
| 0 | 1 | | 2 km | |

16
Woodstock: Dairy Country

Distance: *14.8 miles*
Terrain: *Rolling*
Difficulty: *Moderate*
Recommended bicycle: *Touring/road bike*

This ride doesn't leave the rural town of Woodstock, but you'll pass through four of its villages: Woodstock, North Woodstock, East Woodstock, and South Woodstock. Together these tiny villages are part of a bucolic region of patchwork green hills reminiscent of England's Lake District.

A band of settlers from Roxbury, Massachusetts, founded Woodstock in 1686, just a decade after the Wabbaquasset Indians fled the area during King Philip's War. It was part of the Massachusetts Bay Colony until it joined the Connecticut Colony in 1749.

It began more than 300 years ago as a farming community and for the most part has remained one, a rarity in a state where most farms have been abandoned or converted into country estates. The rolling hills are peppered with the barns and silos of working dairy farms.

Woodstock's green and the grand homes around it reflect its history as a popular 19th-century summer resort for the wealthy, and it still possessses an air of tranquility that suggests life long ago.

One of Woodstock's more colorful residents was Henry Chandler Bowen, a successful dry-goods merchant and publisher of the *Independent,* a pre-Civil War abolitionist newspaper. You can't miss his showy gingerbread 1846 Gothic Revival summer cottage, Roseland, replete with brilliant stained-glass windows and pointed arches. The annual Fourth of July parties at the pink cottage on the green were infamous, attended by several U.S. presidents and other dignitaries. Perhaps nothing stands

Woodstock's verdant hills are dotted with working dairy farms.

out about Bowen's cottage more than its cheery pink hue. It has been painted more than a dozen shades of pink over the past 150 years.

Bowen was also a generous benefactor, restoring Woodstock Academy, creating Roseland Park, and planting hundreds of trees around town. Other attractions around the cottage are its boxwood parterre garden, filled with thousands of flowers in 21 beds, and a carriage barn housing a bowling alley.

The Woodstock Fair in early September, a tradition begun 140 years ago, draws thousands to celebrate the area's agricultural heritage.

Directions for the Ride

Park at the Woodstock Town Hall on CT 169, between the villages of Woodstock and South Woodstock.

0.0 Turn left onto CT 169.

0.5 At the tiny South Woodstock green, turn left onto Roseland Park Road.

2.8 Bear left onto Dugg Hill Road.

3.8 *At the stop sign, go straight onto Dugg Hill Road.*

A short, steep climb passes some of Woodstock's many dairy farms.

5.6 *At the stop sign, turn right onto Chandler School Road.*

6.7 *At the next stop sign, turn right onto Paine District Road.*

8.4 *Turn right onto Hibbard Road.*

9.1 *At the stop sign, go straight onto Woodstock Road.*

In East Woodstock, you'll pass the red post office, an ancient cemetery, the gleaming white spire of the East Woodstock Congregational Church, and a cluster of old clapboard homes.

10.3 *Bear right at the Muddy Brook Fire Department.*

10.8 *At the stop sign, turn left onto CT 169.*

In about 2.5 miles, you'll come to Joy's Country Store, a good stop for ice cream or snacks.

13.9 *The Woodstock green is on the left.*

Other notable buildings surrounding this pristine commons include the 1821 meetinghouse, 1801 Woodstock Academy, and many Revolutionary-era homes. Roseland Cottage is maintained by the Society for the Preservation of New England (860-928-4074) and is open seasonally for tours.

14.8 *Turn left into the Woodstock Town Hall parking lot to end the ride.*

Bicycle Shops

The Silver Bicycle Company, 6 Livery Street, Putnam; 860-928-7370

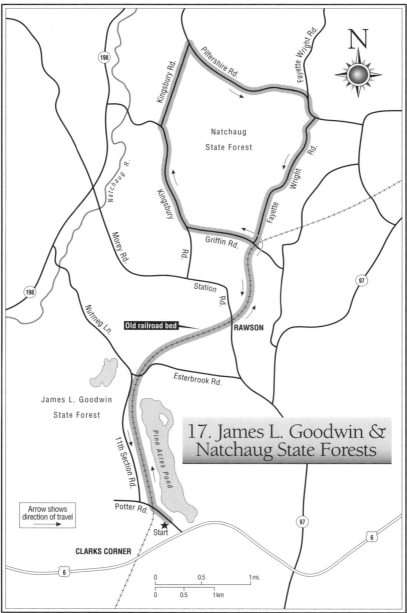

198

Kingsbury Rd.

Pilfershire Rd.

Fayette Wright Rd.

N

Natchaug
State Forest

Kingsbury

Natchaug R.

Wright Rd.

Fayette

Morey Rd.

Rd.

Griffin Rd.

198

Station

Rd.

Nutmeg Ln.

Old railroad bed

RAWSON

97

Esterbrook Rd.

James L. Goodwin

State Forest

11th Section Rd.

Pine Acres Pond

17. James L. Goodwin &
Natchaug State Forests

Arrow shows
direction of travel

Potter Rd.

Start

97

6

CLARKS CORNER

6

| 0 | 0.5 | 1 mi. |
| 0 | 0.5 | 1 km |

17

James L. Goodwin and Natchaug State Forests

Distance: *15.4 miles*
Terrain: *Dirt and paved forest roads; a gravel and dirt railbed*
Difficulty: *Easy*
Recommended bicycle: *Mountain bike*

This pleasant ride passes through an attractive woodland of hardwood trees and towering evergreens in the heart of the state's Quiet Corner. It is actually two state forests: James L. Goodwin State Forest and Conservation Center and the neighboring 12,935-acre Natchaug State Forest to the north. Rolling forest roads and an abandoned railbed take this ride through hilly eastern Connecticut woodlands dotted with numerous marshes, streams, and ponds that are prime wildlife habitats.

The conservation center was the gift of forestry pioneer James L. Goodwin, who donated his clapboard farmhouse and 80 acres of forest to the state in 1964 to educate the public on wildlife issues and forest management. Goodwin, a 1910 graduate of the Yale School of Forestry, originally developed the land as a private tree farm using proper forest management techniques at a time when many of his contemporaries were simply clear-cutting trees.

Today, the 1,820-acre forest, in the towns of Hampton and Chaplin, is bisected by the Airline State Park Trail, a 49-mile abandoned railbed stretching across the northeast corner of the state, from East Hampton to Putnam. The trail follows a route that once connected Boston and New York City and is named for its straight course. The forest is laced with many other trails and wide, easy woodland roads for you to explore, but the blue-blazed Natchaug Trail is closed to mountain bikes.

A peaceful wildlife garden behind the farmhouse is worth a visit, as is

Pine Acres Pond, next to the parking area. A white-blazed hiking trail leads to the edge of the scenic, undeveloped shoreline of this shallow pond, teeming with yellow pond lilies and white water lilies. The trail also leads through a marsh and onto Governor's Island, home to groves of hemlock and pine. A branch of the trail here leads to a wildlife viewing platform. Swallows, kingfishers, and herons reside here, as well as a variety of frogs.

Natchaug State Forest is crisscrossed with trails and broad, smooth forest roads as well as the railbed, which passes through the southeastern corner of this tract. Natchaug stretches into four towns: Chaplin, Hampton, Eastford, and Pomfret. Groves of towering white pines and many marshes and bogs offer a diverse backdrop for this ride. (Be sure to bring bug spray!) On the eastern edge of the state forest you'll pedal through a large marshland, ideal for spotting birds and wildlife in the early morning and evening hours.

This ride is ideal for beginners; the terrain is easy to moderate and can be enjoyed at a leisurely pace. These forests are popular with hikers and equestrians (there's a horse camp and trail system in the Natchaug section), so use caution.

Directions for the Ride

The James L. Goodwin Conservation Center (860-455-9534) is located about 10 miles east of Willimantic on US 6 in Hampton, 3 miles east of the junction of US 6 and CT 198. Look for a brown sign indicating the entrance, which is on Potter Road. The white farmhouse on the left houses the office (860-455-9534), which is open Monday through Friday 9 AM–4 PM. Park on the right side of Potter Road, in the large dirt parking lot just past the boat-launch area overlooking Pine Acres Pond.

0.0 *From the parking area, turn right onto Potter Road, a paved forest road.*

The wildlife garden across from the parking lot has picnic tables and a gazebo if you plan to eat here after the ride.

0.2 *Turn right onto the railbed, passing through a green metal gate.*

This flat, wide trail traverses the woods near 130-acre Pine Acres Pond.

Cyclist and friend in Natchaug State Forest.

1.8 Ride around the gate, cross paved Esterbrook Road (look for the green street sign to the left), climb a short hill, and pass through another green gate to continue on the railbed.

The surface turns to soft gravel on this section of the trail, which passes two marshes and crosses into Natchaug State Forest. *Natchaug* is a Native American word that means "land between the rivers" and refers to the confluence of the Bigelow and Still Rivers just north of the forest. This tract of land was once the hunting grounds of the local Wabbaquasset Indians.

3.2 Pass by another green gate, cross paved Station Road (unmarked), and ride past a row of small boulders to continue on the trail.

Look for a brown CLOSED TO MOTOR VEHICLES sign and a green gate overgrown with brush. You'll pass a weathered brown barn to your right. Shortly thereafter, the grassy railbed leads straight into the woods (the dirt road to the right is a private right-of-way).

4.2 At this green gate, turn left onto Griffin Road (unmarked).

This paved road will soon turn to dirt, and then you'll begin a moderate climb into the woods.

5.0 At the T-intersection, turn right onto Kingsbury Road (unmarked).

This dirt forest road dips up and down wooded hills. You'll pass the main entrance into Natchaug State Forest and a cluster of forest headquarters buildings right before the road becomes paved.

About 0.3 mile past the forest headquarters you'll see a broad picnic area lined with stone walls along the Natchaug River. This is the birthplace of Brig. Gen. Nathaniel Lyon, the first Union general killed in the Civil War—in the battle of Wilson's Creek in 1861. All that's left of the homestead is a stone chimney and fireplace. Lyon is buried in a cemetery along the Natchaug River in the village of Phoenixville, just north of the state forest.

7.4 At the T-intersection at the crest of the hill, turn right onto Pilfershire Road.

This moderately hilly road will turn to dirt just after you pass a quail farm.

9.0 *Turn right onto Fayette Wright Road.*

The road dips down to pass along the edge of Hampton Reservoir, an excellent spot for bird-watching, then rises into the woods past a majestic stand of pine.

11.1 *Where Fayette Wright Road forks, bear left onto paved Griffin Road, then immediately pass through the green gate on the right and ride onto the railbed.*

Follow the railbed back to Goodwin State Forest.

15.1 *At the green gate on Potter Road (it will be the third road the trail crosses), turn left.*

This paved forest road will return to the conservation center parking lot, where the ride ends.

Bicycle Shops

Scott's Cyclery, 1171 Main Street (CT 32), Willimantic; 860-423-8889

The Silver Bicycle Company, 6 Livery Street, Putnam; 860-928-7370

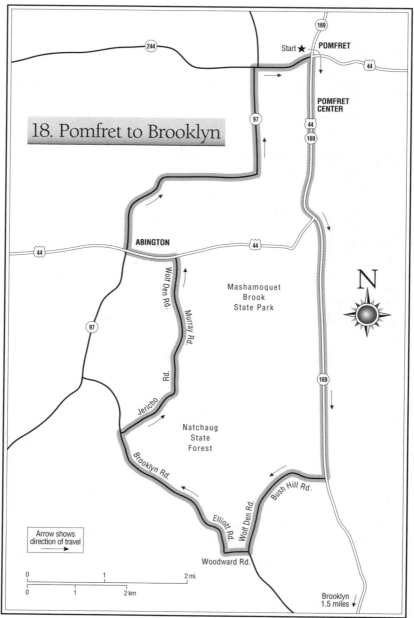

18. Pomfret to Brooklyn

244

169

Start ★ **POMFRET**

44

POMFRET CENTER

97

44

169

ABINGTON

44

44

97

Wolf Den Rd.

Murray Rd.

Mashamoquet
Brook
State Park

169

Rd.

Jericho

Natchaug
State
Forest

Brooklyn Rd.

Bush Hill Rd.

Elliott Rd.

Wolf Den Rd.

Woodward Rd.

Brooklyn
1.5 miles

Arrow shows
direction of travel

0   1   2 mi.
0   1   2 km

N

Paul Woodward, © 2000 The Countryman Press

18
Pomfret to Brooklyn

Distance: *17.8 miles*
Terrain: *Low to moderate hills*
Difficulty: *Moderate*
Recommended bicycle: *Touring/road bike*

The section of CT 169 from Norwich to Woodstock is deemed one of the "10 most outstanding scenic byways" in the country. The annual pageant of color in New England is perhaps the best of all natural events, and people travel far to see the foliage that is particularly stunning in the Quiet Corner.

This scenic ride passes through the National Heritage Corridor of the Quinebaug and Shetucket River Valley, 544,000 acres of preserved villages and green space that has been called "the last green valley" in the megalopolis stretching from Boston to Washington, D.C. This rural area is dotted with quiet towns, patchwork rolling hills of emerald fields, orchards tufted with pink and white blossoms, Colonial farmhouses, and bright red barns surrounded by the thick woods of Natchaug State Forest and Mashamoquet State Park. The whole of it is crisscrossed with ribbons of road perfect for cycling.

Those who settled Pomfret in 1713 cleared hilltops and ridges for farming. The sunny higher elevation meant a longer growing season than in the low valleys shaded by steep hills, which were often in danger of flooding from rivers and streams. Many of the Colonial houses and barns of these upland farms still dot the hillsides much as they did then. The town green is home to two exclusive private schools, Pomfret School and the Rectory.

In the 18th century, Pomfret was home to Israel Putnam, one of the state's most lauded folk heroes, both for his illustrious military service and for continuously proving his mettle.

The Quiet Corner abounds in pastoral scenes.

Putnam's family was among the first settlers of the Massachusetts Bay Colony. He came to Connecticut in 1739 and began farming in the Mortlake section of Pomfret. His rough ways didn't make him popular with Pomfret's gentry, however, until the winter of 1743. According to legend, he won them over by killing a rogue wolf that was ravaging the livestock herds of neighboring farmers. It was believed to be the last wolf in Connecticut.

The lore surrounding "Old Put" continued into his service in the French and Indian War, the Battle of Bunker Hill, and his command of the Continental Army's winter quarters in Redding (now a state park; see ride 23). Apparently, he left his oxen and plow in the middle of a furrow in his field in the rush to Lexington. Legend also has Putnam escaping the British in 1779 by riding his horse down a cliff in the Horse Neck section of Greenwich—when he was in his sixties. He returned to Pomfret and lived 10 more quiet years until his death in 1790.

Directions for the Ride

Park at the Vanilla Bean Café at the junction of CT 169 and US 44 with CT 97.

0.0 *Make a left turn out of the parking lot. At the stop sign, turn right onto CT 169/US 44.*

Pass the sprawling prep school campuses of the Rectory and the Pomfret School, set amid centuries-old homes tucked in this upland area of hills and forests. After passing the Pomfret School, you will begin a steep descent.

2.0 *Follow the road as it bears left.*

2.2 *US 44 and CT 169 split here; follow CT 169 to the left.*

2.8 *At the traffic light (the junction of CT 101), go straight onto CT 169.*

You'll cross into Brooklyn in about 2 miles.

5.7 *Turn right onto Bush Hill Road.*

This road is lined on both sides with majestic trees and ancient stone walls.

6.7 *At the stop sign, bear left onto Wolf Den Road.*

At this rural crossroads is Hillandale Farm, home to one of the state's finest and most romantic restaurants. Eating at the Golden Lamb Buttery (860-774-4423) is a unique experience, to say the least. In warm-weather months, guests are serenaded on a hayride before dining in the barn. The cuisine is highly praised by food critics; consequently, the one dinner seating books months in advance. The restaurant is also open for lunch.

7.4 *Turn right onto Woodward Road.*

7.6 *Turn right onto Elliott Road.*

You'll ride through Natchaug State Forest and cross back into Pomfret.

9.5 *At the stop sign, turn right onto Brooklyn Road.*

9.9 *Turn right onto Jericho Road.*

This will turn into Wolf Den Road as it passes through Mashamoquet Brook State Park.

12.7 At the stop sign, turn left onto US 44.

Directly across the intersection is Pete's Drive-In, a popular seasonal roadside eatery.

13.4 At the traffic light, turn right onto CT 97.

The white clapboard Rucki's General Store is the genuine article, on the corner of US 44 and CT 97.

15.7 Follow CT 97 as it turns left.

17.0 Bear right onto CT 97.

17.8 The ride ends as you return to the Vanilla Bean Café.

Bicycle Shops

Al's Ordinary Bike Shop, 21 Furnace Street, Danielson; 860-774-1660

The Silver Bicycle Company, 6 Livery Street, Putnam; 860-928-7370

19

Windham to Lebanon:
A New England Village Tour

Distance: 61.3 miles (48 miles excluding the loop to Lebanon)
Terrain: Rolling hills with several steep climbs, especially on the Lebanon section
Difficulty: Strenuous
Recommended bicycle: Touring/road bike

On this tour—which can be completed in one day or stretched into two—you'll pedal through several New England postcard scenes: the village greens of Windham, Canterbury, and Lebanon, and the pastoral countryside that connects them. In these Connecticut towns, the green is a historic landscape marking where colonists settled, built a meetinghouse, grazed their livestock, and gathered for public activitites.

Windham was the hub of political activity in the northeast corner when it became the county seat in 1726. The village's political roots go further back, however, to its first town meeting on June 12, 1692. Windham actively provided the Continental Army with men and supplies, and it must have been a proud moment for its citizens when Gen. Rochambeau and his troops marched by the green during the Revolution.

The gracious sound of Hampton's name evokes images of austerity, which you'll see in the handsome antique homes lining the village streets. The black-shuttered Hampton General Store sits across from the soaring spire of the Hampton Congregational Church, Connecticut's second-oldest meetinghouse.

The cornerstone of the Canterbury green is the Prudence Crandall House. Crandall, a Quaker from Rhode Island, ran a private school in her home and caused public outrage by admitting a local black girl. Her response was to open a school exclusively for "young ladies and little

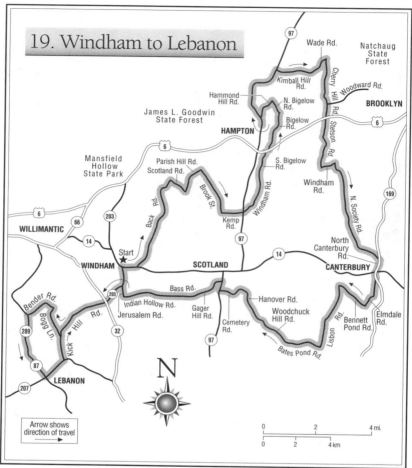

19. Windham to Lebanon

Paul Woodward, © 2000 The Countryman Press

misses of color" in 1833. The state's general assembly in turn passed the infamous "Black Law," which prohibited the education of black students from out of state. Crandall faced harassment by an angry mob of residents who vandalized the school; she ultimately spent a night in prison. In a stroke of irony, Crandall is now considered a heroine.

History buffs won't want to miss the side trip to the Lebanon green. Its mile-long hilltop common, one of the largest in New England, is cared for by people who live around it, some of whom descend from the original farmers who settled the land.

During the Revolution, Lebanon was a thriving community on one of the main routes between Boston and New York. Resident Jonathan Trumbull was an ardent patriot and the only colonial governor to openly support the American Revolution. His red clapboard mercantile store became the Revolutionary War Office, where Washington, Lafayette, Rochambeau, and other military leaders met to plan strategy. More than 1,000 meetings were held in this small frame building on the green, and Connecticut became known as "the Provision State" in part because of Trumbull's efforts to supply Washington's army. Trumbull was one of Washington's closest friends and advisors, whom the future president called "Brother Jonathan."

Other illustrious Lebanon residents were William Williams, signer of the Declaration of Independence, and Trumbull's son John, whose paintings of war scenes are on the dollar bill.

Directions for the Ride

This tour begins in Windham, at the small green in the village center. You can park along the west side of the green in front of the Windham Library.

0.0 *From the green, pass in front of the old Windham Inn and go east on Scotland Road (CT 14).*

> The quaint green is surrounded by buildings centuries old, including a c. 1790 sheriff's office and the 1832 Greek Revival Windham Free Library.

0.6 *Turn left onto Back Road.*

> This relatively flat wooded road will bring you across the Chaplin town line.

3.0 *At the Y-intersection, bear left to continue on Back Road (Parish Hill Road climbs to the right).*

4.5 *At the stop sign, turn right onto Scotland Road (unmarked).*

5.3 *At the next stop sign, turn left onto Parish Hill Road.*

> You will pass an old homestead surrounded by orchards and then descend Parish Hill into the town of Hampton.

6.4 Turn right onto Brook Street.

8.3 At the stop sign, turn left onto Kemp Road (unmarked).
Climb about 0.5 mile to hilltop cornfields.

9.1 At the stop sign, turn left. At the next stop sign, go straight across CT 97.

9.7 Bear left onto Bigelow Road (unmarked).

11.4 At the Y-intersection, bear right onto South Bigelow Road.

11.8 At this stop sign, turn right onto busy US 6 for a very short distance. Take the first left to continue on Bigelow Road.

12.7 At the stop sign, continue straight.

14.0 At the intersection where you are facing a brown, two-story clapboard house, bear left, then make a sharp right onto Hammond Hill Road.
After a steep descent, a climb through picturesque farmland will take you to the village of Hampton.

14.9 At the stop sign, turn left onto CT 97.
The Hampton General Store sells everything from groceries to livestock feed; it also has a deli. Ride as far as the Hampton town offices to get a full glimpse of the architecture this village has to offer, then turn around and head north on CT 97.

15.0 At the stop sign, continue straight on CT 97.

18.5 Turn right onto Kimball Hill Road.
This climb up Kimball Hill will reward you with views of hilltop meadows, cornfields, and distant hills.

As you descend the other side and cross into Pomfret, look for the sprawling red barns and rustic stone and wood fences of Sharpe Hill Vineyard (860-974-3549). This small but well-regarded winery, complete with a taproom and wine garden, is open to the public 11–5 Friday through Sunday.

21.6 At the stop sign, turn right onto Cherry Hill Road (unmarked).

23.5 At the Y-intersection, bear right (Woodward Road goes to the left) and head toward US 6.

23.9 At the blinking traffic light, cross US 6 and onto Stetson Road.

The 1735 Jonathan Trumbull house on Lebanon's mile-long hilltop green.

Mik-Ran's Sugar House (860-774-7926) offers demonstrations of maple syrup production in February and March; the gift shop sells maple syrup, candy, and butter.

26.0 At the stop sign, turn left onto Windham Road.

26.5 Turn right onto North Society Road (unmarked).

This gently rolling road will bring you into the town of Canterbury.

31.1 At the stop sign, turn right onto North Canterbury Road (CT 169).

31.6 At this stop sign, you are at the junction of CT 169/CT 14, which marks the center of Canterbury.

The clapboard house across the intersection is the Prudence Crandall Museum; built in 1805, it is one of the sites on the Connecticut Freedom Trail. The museum (860-546-9916) has exhibits on black history, the abolitionist movement, and women's rights. It's open Wednesday through Sunday 10–4:30, February to mid-December. The town green is a National Historic District, with more than 32 historically or architecturally significant 18th-century buildings. The oldest house on the green is the First Parsonage, where Benedict Arnold was a student.

31.9 *Continue on CT 169, then shortly bear right onto Elmdale Road.*

33.1 *At the stop sign, turn right onto Bennett Pond Road.*

34.5 *Turn left at this stop sign onto Lisbon Road.*

37.0 *At the stop sign, turn right onto Bates Pond Road.*

38.2 *Cross Water Street at the stop sign.*

39.6 *At the bottom of a very steep descent, turn left onto Cemetery Road.*

41.3 *Turn left again to continue on Cemetery Road.*

42.2 *At the stop sign, turn right onto CT 97.*

42.5 *Turn left onto Gager Hill Road.*

This is an area of working farms, evidenced by the seemingly endless acres of cornfields on both sides of the road.

44.5 *Continue straight onto Bass Road. (At the far end, this road will be marked Indian Hollow Road.)*

46.6 *At the stop sign, turn right onto Jerusalem Road.*

This is where you'll have to choose whether to continue the tour or return on the shortcut to Windham.

To return to Windham: Bear right and follow Windham Center Road (CT 203) for just under a mile to the Windham green.

To continue to Lebanon: Turn left onto CT 203.

47.9 *Cross the Shetucket River, then cross Windham Road (CT 32) at the traffic light.*

Pass through the old mill village of South Windham and begin the strenuous climb up Machine Shop Hill, which will turn into Kick Hill Road as you cross the Lebanon town line. This is one of the ride's most challenging sections.

50.3 *Turn right onto Chappell Road and immediately turn right onto Bogg Lane.*

As you descend this rural road you will have a stunning view of the hills and farms scattered throughout Lebanon.

51.4 *Turn left onto Bender Road.*
This is a hard-packed dirt road for 0.5 mile.

51.9 *At the stop sign, continue straight on Bender Road (the surface returns to pavement here).*

52.7 *At this stop sign, turn left onto Beaumont Highway (CT 289).*

54.4 *At the Lebanon green, turn left at the stop sign, then make an immediate right onto West Town Street.*
Lebanon's common is lined with widely spaced antique homes, among them 30 historic buildings and sites. In addition to the War Office, they include the 1760 home of Dr. William Beaumont, regarded as the "father of physiology," who did many of his pioneering studies on soldiers during the Revolution. The Wadsworth Stable can claim George Washington's horse among its more famous boarders. Near the stable is the 1735 Jonathan Trumbull House, which is open to visitors Tuesday through Saturday 1–5, mid-May through mid-October.

55.3 *At the end of the green, turn left at the stop sign, passing the redbrick Old Lebanon Meeting House.*

55.4 *At the blinking traffic light, head straight on Exeter Road (CT 207).*

56.3 *Just past the Lebanon Elementary School, turn left onto Kick Hill Road.*

56.6 *At the stop sign, continue straight.*
Retrace your way to South Windham here.

59.5 *Go straight at the stop sign through South Windham.*

59.6 *At the traffic light, go straight to follow CT 203 north to Windham.*

60.5 *At the stop sign, bear left to continue onto CT 203.*

61.3 *The tour ends at the Windham green.*

Bicycle Shops

Al's Ordinary Bike Shop, 21 Furnace Street, Danielson; 860-774-1660

Scott's Cyclery, 1171 Main Street (CT 32), Willimantic; 860-423-8889

Nearby B&Bs

Friendship Valley, 60 Pomfret Road (CT 169), Brooklyn; 860-779-9696

Tannerbrook B&B, 329 Pomfret Road (CT 169), Brooklyn; 860-774-4822

Woodchuck B&B, 256 Cemetery Road, Canterbury; 860-546-1278

Nathan Fuller House, 147 Plains Road, Scotland; 860-456-0687

20
Pachaug State Forest

Distance: 8.8 miles
Terrain: Gently rolling dirt roads
Difficulty: Moderate
Recommended bicycle: Mountain bike

Connecticut's largest state forest encompasses 30,000 heavily wooded acres dotted with lakes, streams, and rocky ridgelines spread across six towns. The bulk of this vast tract lies in Voluntown, where the forest headquarters are located. *Pachaug* is a Native American word that means "bend in the river," referring to the Pachaug River, which runs through the forest from Beach Pond to the Quinebaug River.

This area was once inhabited by the Narragansett, Pequot, and Mohegan tribes. The Mohegans, aided by colonists, defeated the other two groups in the late 1600s. In 1700 a small tract of land here was given to veterans of the Indian War, thus the area became known as "Volunteer's Town," later Voluntown in 1721.

At one time, this massive woodland tract was farmland and pasture, as evidenced by the old cellar holes and miles of stone walls twisting through the hills and along the roads. A mill industry grew up along the ponds and streams, starting with the first mill in 1711. Trees have reclaimed the land here, an oak-hickory forest with groves of white pine, red pine, and hemlock. The reforestation has caused a resurgence of deer, pheasant, fox, rabbits, and grouse, among other species. Hunting is allowed here, so check at headquarters if you're not familiar with Connecticut's hunting season. If you ride during hunting season, wear bright clothing and call out if you see hunters in the area.

Bikes are allowed only on the dirt roads and snowmobile trails. If you plan to hike here, don't miss the trail leading to Pachaug's highest point,

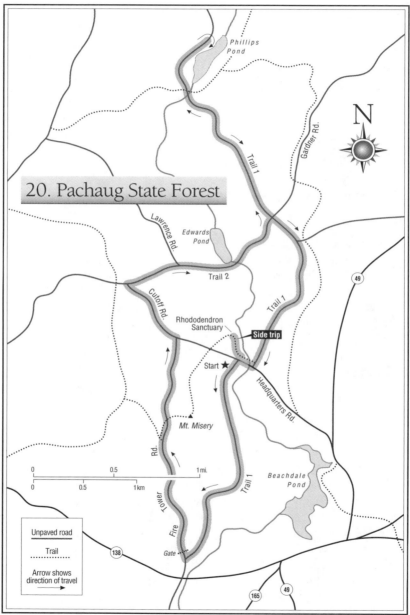

20. Pachaug State Forest

Phillips Pond

Gardner Rd.

Trail 1

N

Lawrence Rd.

Edwards Pond

Trail 2

Cutoff Rd.

Trail 1

49

Rhododendron Sanctuary

Side trip

Start ★

Headquarters Rd.

Rd.

Mt. Misery

Tower

Beachdale Pond

Fire

0   0.5   1 mi.
0   0.5   1 km

Trail 1

Gate

138

165   49

Unpaved road

Trail

Arrow shows
direction of travel

Paul Woodward, © 2000 The Countryman Press

the 441-foot bald-rock summit of Mount Misery, which offers expansive views of Connecticut's eastern hills and ridges. The trailhead can be picked up on Fire Tower Road or at the Mount Misery camping area.

A jewel in this state forest is the Rhododendron Sanctuary, one of only a few such refuges in New England. This unique coniferous swamp is full of Atlantic white cedar, hemlock, and giant rhododendron, which is rare in Connecticut. The flowers of this shrub are in full bloom from mid-June to mid-July, when the profuse blooms crowd the edge of the trail. The thick woody branches of these evergreen shrubs reach nearly 20 feet high.

If you enjoy rustic camping, the Mount Misery campground has 22 wooded sites and the Green Falls campground has 18 sites; there is also a horse camp in the Frog Hollow Area. Doug's Place is a scenic picnic area just inside the forest entrance, on the shore of Beachdale Pond.

The Green Falls Recreation Area is also part of the forest; take CT 138 east from exit 85 off I-395. The forest entrance is 8.3 miles east on CT 138.

Food and supplies can be purchased in Voluntown near the junction of CT 49 and CT 138, just before the park entrance. A small grocery store and pizza restaurant are also here.

Directions for the Ride

This ride begins in the Mount Misery Recreation Area of Pachaug State Forest (860-376-4075). From I-395, take exit 85, follow CT 138 for 6.2 miles, and turn left on CT 49 north; the forest entrance is 0.5 mile farther on the left. Take Headquarters Road into the forest and park at the boulder-lined ball field near the information kiosk and pay phone.

0.0 *Facing the ball field, go left onto Trail 1.*

> This 2,000-acre section of the forest is dedicated to Herman Haupt Chapman, a professor of the Yale School of Forestry.

1.7 *Just after passing two small green posts, turn right onto Fire Tower Road, a gated, unmarked fire road.*

> This quiet, wooded road gradually climbs into the woods, then descends past a clearing.

2.5 *At the Y-junction in the trail, bear right.*

Connecticut's largest state forest is laced with dirt roads and trails.

This sandy road has a grassy median and pockets of loose rock.

2.7 *Pass through another gate and continue straight.*

3.3 *Turn left at this T-intersection.*

Begin a long, fairly steep climb here.

3.8 *At the next junction, turn right onto Trail 2 (look for a small brown signpost to the left).*

Begin a fun, fast descent here.

4.3 *Continue straight on Trail 2 (Lawrence Road goes to the left here).*

Soon you'll pass Edwards Pond on the left, a swampy area teeming with wildlife.

5.1 *At this four-way intersection, turn left onto Trail 1.*

6.3 *Arrive at Phillips Pond and its small picnic area.*

From here, you'll backtrack to Trail 1.

7.5 *Back at the four-way junction, continue straight on Trail 1.*

7.7 *Cross a brook; just past it on the left is the Lowden Brook Picnic Area. Shortly thereafter, bear right.*

8.6 *Pass through a green gate.*

Ride through a youth camp area, exiting through two stone gateposts.

8.7 *Bear right and cross a small bridge.*

8.8 *The ride ends at the ball field.*

Side Trip: To ride to the Rhododendron Sanctuary, take the marked trail that is about 20 yards from the ball field, on the right. Follow this narrow gravel path for about 0.25 mile into the swampy wooded area, ending at a wood boardwalk and observation platform. Return on the same trail.

Bicycle Shops

Al's Ordinary Bike Shop, 21 Furnace Street, Danielson; 860-774-1660

Groton Cyclery, 1360 CT 184, Groton; 860-445-6745

Rose City Cycle, Inc., 427 West Main Street (CT 82), Norwich; 860-887-7442

21
The Thompson Green

Distance: *7.5 miles*
Terrain: *One moderately challenging climb; flat roads around West Thompson Lake*
Difficulty: *Moderate*
Recommended bicycle: *Touring/road bike*

The hilltop village of Thompson sits at the junction of CT 193 and CT 200, much closer to I-395 than it seems. Many handsome 19th century homes and buildings, including a private school and an inn, surround the neat common and reflect the prosperity that blessed its residents.

The rambling White Horse Inn at Vernon Stiles is the cornerstone of the village. It's named for Capt. Vernon Stiles, who opened the establishment as a stagecoach tavern in 1814. Many young couples from Rhode Island and Massachusetts purportedly fled from the stringent laws of their home states to be married at the tavern, with Captain Stiles officiating. The inn is now a restaurant.

The railroad passed Thompson by—likely due to its hilltop location—and saved the village from the rapid development that befell most other communities. The green is among the most serene and classic in the state and is lovingly cared for by the Village Improvement Society, organized in 1874.

This out-and-back ride begins at the dam on scenic West Thompson Lake and climbs CT 93 to the green. Food and services can be found in Putnam, southeast of Thompson on US 44.

The lake, managed by the U.S. Army Corps of Engineers, is surrounded by 1,672 acres of open land, forest, and wetlands that attract many migratory birds. There are picnic shelters and campsites around the lake as well as hiking trails. If you're interested in mountain biking,

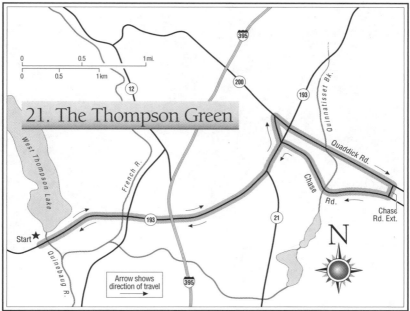

21. The Thompson Green

Paul Woodward, © 2000 The Countryman Press

the staff at the Silver Bicycle Company (see Bicycle Shops) can assist with planning a ride here.

Directions for the Ride

West Thompson Lake is off I-395, exit 99. Take CT 200 to Grosvenor Dale, then head south on CT 12 and follow signs to the West Thompson Dam. Park at the white garage on West Thompson Road, near the dam's gatehouse.

0.0 *Turn left out of the parking lot and take West Thompson Road across the dam at West Thompson Lake.*

The dam lies on the Quinebaug River, just upstream from its confluence with the French River, one of six dams in the Thames River basin that help control flooding in the area from the Thames River to Long Island Sound.

0.8 *Use caution when crossing the railroad tracks here.*

Connecticut's northeast corner is noted for its quiet country roads.

0.9 *At the traffic light, go straight onto Thompson Road (CT 193).*

Begin the long, gradual climb to the village of Thompson.

2.4 *At the green, turn left onto Chase Road.*

This road circles the green past the prep-school campus of Marianapolis. The Thompson Hill Gallery, across the green at 355 Thompson Road, showcases traditional and contemporary original art.

2.7 *At the stop sign, turn right onto CT 200.*

The White Horse Inn at Vernon Stiles (860-923-9571) is a highly regarded restaurant in a former inn on the tip of the green.

2.8 *At the blinking red light, go straight onto Quaddick Road.*

3.8 *Turn right onto Chase Road Extension.*

These roads will take you through a quiet neighborhood behind the green.

3.9 *Turn right onto Chase Road.*

5.2 *At the stop sign, turn left onto Thompson Road (CT 193).*

6.8 At the traffic light, go straight onto West Thompson Road.

7.5 After passing West Thompson Lake, turn right into the parking lot to end the ride.

Bicycle Shops

The Silver Bicycle Company, 6 Livery Street, Putnam; 860-928-7370

THE HOUSATONIC
AND CONNECTICUT
RIVER VALLEYS

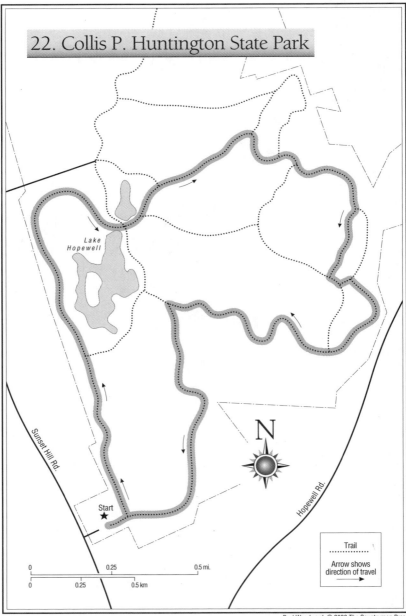

22. Collis P. Huntington State Park

*Lake
Hopewell*

Sunset Hill Rd

Hopewell Rd.

Start
★

N

| 0 | | 0.25 | | 0.5 mi. |
| 0 | 0.25 | | 0.5 km | |

Trail
....

Arrow shows
direction of travel
———▶

Paul Woodward, © 2000 The Countryman Press

22
Collis P. Huntington State Park

Distance: *A 4.5-mile loop (can be extended with the many additional trails here)*
Terrain: *Easy to moderate forest roads and doubletrack trails*
Difficulty: *Moderate*
Recommended bicycle: *Mountain bike*

This beautiful 878-acre park in the rural town of Redding is a great place to explore. It was given to Connecticut by the poet Archer Huntington and his wife, the noted sculptor Anna Hyatt Huntington, in memory of Archer Huntington's stepfather, Collis P. Huntington, a wealthy railroad magnate and philanthropist. The secluded, well-worn paths are used by cyclists, hikers, and equestrians; the stocked ponds are popular fishing spots.

Anna Hyatt Huntington's artistry graces the trailhead at the unmarked park entrance on Sunset Hill Road. Visitors are greeted by two lively bronze wildlife sculptures: on the right, a mother bear with two cubs, and on the left, a pair of howling wolves.

For a relatively small park, the landscape is surprisingly diverse. The hills and ravines are thick with mountain laurel. If you ride here in June you will be treated to their abundant pink and white blossoms; at other times of year look for their telltale clusters of dark green leaves. Dramatic rock outcrops overlook many of the trails, large glacial boulders are scattered among the hills, and the lowland bogs support ferns and other lush vegetation. Wooden boardwalks cross the many streams that feed into Lake Hopewell, South Pond, and East and West Lagoons.

Exploring this rocky terrain brings to mind the land the earliest settlers were faced with and the sheer volume of rock they pulled from the earth to fashion into stone walls to mark the boundaries of their fields.

This densely wooded park and its network of easily rideable dirt roads and trails will appeal to riders of all ability levels. You can make short, easy loops around the ponds or explore the park for hours by riding different combinations of trails. Most of them are hard packed and have areas of loose rock, exposed gnarled roots, and many short climbs and descents to make it interesting. The loop is crossed everywhere by unmarked paths, which are also open to mountain bikes. Many of the old carriage roads around the lakes are flat and easy; the singletrack trails are more technical.

Directions for the Ride

From CT 302 in Bethel, go south on Putnam Park Road (CT 58), then turn left onto Sunset Hill Road. The unmarked park entrance is designated by two stone gateposts. The park is about 4.5 miles from downtown Bethel and about 8 miles southeast of Danbury. From Danbury, take CT 53 to CT 302, then take CT 58 south to the park. From the south, take exit 45 off the Merritt Parkway (CT 15) to CT 58; in Redding, turn right onto Sunset Hill Road.

0.0 *From the parking lot, pass between the two sculptures and follow the narrow dirt trail to the left toward a hilltop meadow.*

The trail cuts through a beautiful open field of tall grass. The expansive views of distant ridges will soon disappear as you quickly descend toward the woods.

0.1 *At the T-intersection, turn left.*

The trail becomes wide doubletrack here and gets brushy, but it remains relatively open. You'll follow the base of the meadow for a short time, which is separated from the trail by an old stone wall.

0.6 *At this intersection, continue straight.*

The woods are dense here, crisscrossed with stone walls. The trail starts to descend gradually, and in about 0.5 mile passes remnants of a couple of stone buildings on your right, just as you pass a paddock on the left. You can also catch glimpses of Lake Hopewell through the trees below as you continue downhill.

1.1 *At the Y-intersection, bear right and continue descending into the woods.*

Soon after passing a stone foundation on the left, you'll go past a small, wooden-plank bridge on the left. Continue straight and cross a wider bridge.

1.4 Bear left at the small grassy clearing.

There are ponds on both sides of the trail here. When you continue away from the clearing, you'll have a pond on your left and woods to the right.

1.5 At this Y-intersection, bear right and continue descending into thick, lush woods.

To the left you'll see a wooden boardwalk crossing a stream.

1.8 At the next junction, bear right onto a trail marked with red blazes.

To the left you'll see a narrower trail—marked with a yellow blaze with a "K"—that climbs a hill.

2.1 Bear right at the Y-intersection, continuing on the red-blazed trail; make an immediate left onto the white-blazed trail.

A yellow-blazed trail marked with an "L" leads to the left.

2.2 Turn right onto the blue-blazed trail.

Pass by an enormous rock ledge on the right and a large boulder on the left. Shortly you'll cross a stream on a plank bridge and then descend farther into the woods. Continue straight as you pass two narrow paths to a trailhead on the left. Ride through a lush bog, make two stream crossings on wooden bridges, and then climb this twisting trail out of the bog.

2.7 At the Y, bear left and continue following the blue blazes.

You'll make two more moderately challenging ascents linked by easier flat sections, winding around the base of a large rock outcropping.

3.3 At this three-way intersection, marked with a white "R," bear left onto the blue-blazed trail and immediately cross a wooden-plank bridge.

4.0 South Pond is on your right. Cross the wooden bridge and bear right to follow the shore for a short time, then climb a short, steep hill.

The trail suddenly becomes unmarked, steep, and strewn with exposed roots and rocks. Follow this heavily eroded trail away from the pond; your technical skills will determine whether you ride or walk your bike.

4.5 *Turn left to return to the singletrack that climbs past the meadow to end the ride, or continue straight to reenter the woods and explore more trails.*

Bicycle Shops

Bethel Cycle & Fitness, 120 Greenwood Avenue (CT 302), Bethel; 203-792-4640

23
Newtown to Weir Farm

Distance: 41 miles
Terrain: Rolling to steep hills; one 1.5-mile dirt road
Difficulty: Strenuous
Recommended bicycle: Touring/road bike

This ride passes through some of the more peaceful yet hilly sections of this largely developed area of the state. It may surprise some cyclists to find themselves on unpaved Poverty Hollow Road, which rivals some of the most scenic country lanes in the state's northern reaches.

You'll begin the ride in the colonial village of Newtown, whose grand lineup of beautifully restored homes along Main Street is tarnished only by the unfortunate drone of traffic that rolls through the center of town. The centerpiece of this historic avenue is the 200-year-old red clapboard general store.

One of only two national parks in the country recognizing American art is on a pastoral hilltop in Wilton, which you'll encounter on the next leg of the ride. Weir Farm National Historic Site was the summer retreat of noted American Impressionist painter Julian Alden Weir. He turned the 153-acre farm into an artists' retreat in the late 1800s, where artists like John Singer Sargent, Childe Hassam, and John Henry Twachtman painted the rural landscape of meadows, woodlands, and rambling stone walls. This beautiful estate, which has been called the American equivalent of Giverney, draws artists, photographers, and nature lovers inspired by the surroundings.

Next you'll travel narrow winding roads through Redding to discover grand estates tucked into perfectly manicured grounds, enclaves of well-tended privacy. The town figures prominently in Revolutionary War history. On the site that is now Putnam Memorial State Park, about 3,100

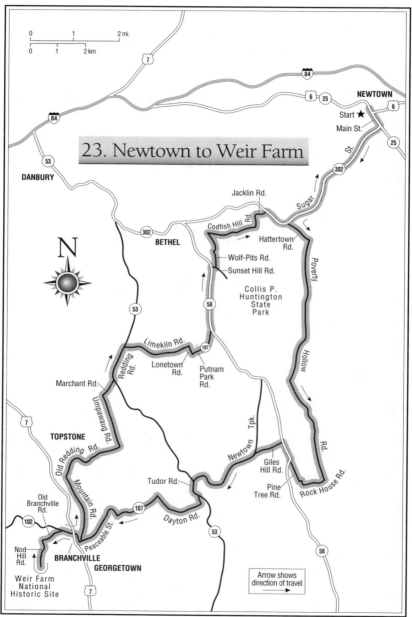

0 1 2 mi.
0 1 2 km

7

84

6 25 **NEWTOWN**

6

Start ★

Main St.

25

302

Sugar St.

23. Newtown to Weir Farm

53

DANBURY

Jacklin Rd.

302

Codfish Hill Rd.

BETHEL

Hattertown Rd.

Wolf-Pits Rd.

Sunset Hill Rd.

Poverty

Collis P.
Huntington
State
Park

N

53

58

Limekiln Rd.

107

Hollow

Redding Rd.

Lonetown Rd.

Putnam
Park
Rd.

Marchant Rd.

Umpawaug Rd.

7

TOPSTONE

Old Redding Rd.

Newtown Tpk.

Giles
Hill Rd.

Rd.

Tudor Rd.

Pine
Tree Rd.

Rock House Rd.

Old
Branchville
Rd.

Mountain Rd.

102

107

Dayton Rd.

53

Nod
Hill
Rd.

Peaceable St.

BRANCHVILLE

GEORGETOWN

58

Weir Farm
National
Historic Site

7

Arrow shows
direction of travel
→

Paul Woodward, © 2000 The Countryman Press

men in Washington's Northern Army camped here under the command of Gen. Israel Putnam (see ride 18) during the harsh winter of 1778–79. The encampment known as Putnam's Valley Forge was strategically located an equal distance between Washington's Hudson River headquarters and Long Island Sound.

Local history and landmarks are depicted in hand-painted wall murals in Newtown's Edmond Town Hall, but the building's most unique feature is its one-screen movie theater. Time your ride right and you can return to Main Street in time to catch a current release. Call the Edmond Town Hall Theatre (860-426-2475) for show times.

Directions for the Ride

This tour begins on Main Street at Edmond Town Hall, next to the Newtown General Store, where you can pick up sandwiches, snacks, and drinks. To get there from I-84, take exit 10; follow US 6 west and then CT 25 north to Newtown. Parking is available in the lot behind the town hall.

0.0 *From the town hall, turn right onto Main Street (CT 25).*

Pass the general store, the Newtown Congregational Church (according to local legend, the rooster weathervane was used as a target by French soldiers encamped here during the Revolution in 1781), some of Main Street's elegant homes, and its landmark soaring flagpole, erected in 1876.

0.5 *At the traffic light next to the police station, turn right onto Sugar Street (CT 302).*

This is a fairly busy road connecting Newtown and Bethel. You'll pass a few farms; however, most farmland here has been developed into home sites.

3.8 *Turn left onto Hattertown Road.*

Look for a green signpost on the right pointing to Bethel and Danbury.

4.4 *At the stop sign, turn right onto Poverty Hollow Road.*

This road gradually descends all the way to Easton. First you'll pass a mix of horse farms, new homes, and fine old homesteads. As you descend, you'll find yourself on a secluded rural road that many people would be surprised to see in suburban Fairfield County.

8.2 **When you arrive at a tiny grassy triangle across from a handsome white clapboard Colonial, continue straight on Poverty Hollow Road (Church Hill Road goes to the right here).**

9.1 **Follow Poverty Hollow Road to the right, past a yellow NO WINTER MAINTENANCE sign. The pavement will end shortly.**

This hard-packed dirt road is passable on a road bike. The last leg of this road cuts through a remote forest.

10.5 **At the stop sign, turn right onto paved Rock House Road (unmarked).**

This turns into Pine Tree Road at the Redding town line, twisting uphill into the woods.

11.8 **At the stop sign, turn right onto CT 58 (unmarked).**

Shortly you'll pass the Spinning Wheel Inn and turn left onto Giles Hill Road.

13.1 **At the Y, bear left on Newtown Turnpike.**

When the water is high, you can hear the Little River rushing by on the left.

13.2 **At the stop sign, bear left to continue on Newtown Turnpike (unmarked).**

Soon you'll glimpse the Saugatuck Reservoir through the trees. The road ahead hugs the shoreline.

15.1 **At the stop sign, go straight onto CT 53.**

15.5 **Turn right onto Tudor Road.**

Begin a steep climb here.

15.7 **Turn right onto Dayton Road.**

The climb continues and then becomes more gradual before descending.

17.0 **At the stop sign, turn left onto CT 107.**

18.1 **Turn right onto Peaceable Street.**

Look carefully for this very narrow hilly road; it starts on a sharp bend in the road.

Weir Farm: A national historic site nestled among wooded hills in Wilton.

19.7 *At the stop sign, turn right onto Portland Street. Cross the railroad tracks at the Branchville train station, ride through the parking lot, and bear left onto the narrow road heading toward US 7.*

In the small depot building, the Whistle Stop Bakery & Café serves baked goods, snacks, and drinks.

19.8 *At the traffic light, cross US 7 onto Branchville Road (CT 102).*

20.3 *Turn left onto Old Branchville Road. (You'll see a brown sign for the Weir Farm National Historic Site.)*

This is a long, steep climb.

20.8 *Continue left onto Nod Hill Road (look for a small brown sign on the right).*

21.5 *At the Y-intersection, bear left onto Nod Hill Road (Pelham Road goes to the right) at Weir Farm National Historic Site.*

Bikes are not allowed on the preserve, so lock them in the bike rack across the street from the Burlingham House Visitor Center. You can take a guided tour of the grounds and art studios or explore the trails and dirt roads on your own. (Keep in mind that

Weir's Greek Revival farmhouse is a private residence.) Don't miss the Weir Farm Historic Painting Sites Trail, which features the actual landscapes that inspired the famous paintings. The grounds are open daily; the visitors center is open Wednesday through Sunday.

22.3 At the stop sign, turn right onto Old Branchville Road.

22.8 At the stop sign, turn right onto Branchville Road (CT 102).

23.0 At the traffic light, cross US 7 and ride through the train station parking lot.

23.1 Cross the railroad tracks and go straight up Portland Street.

23.2 Turn left on Peaceable Street.

23.3 Turn left on Mountain Road.

You'll make a steep climb followed by a winding descent.

25.0 At the stop sign, turn right onto Old Redding Road.

Use caution while climbing this steep, winding road; the turns are very tight.

26.8 At the stop sign, turn left onto Umpawaug Road.

This steep hill is lined on both sides with elegant country estates set on perfectly manicured lawns.

28.1 Bear right onto Marchant Road.

Just around this sharp bend is a tiny redbrick schoolhouse, the Umpawaug School, where local schoolchildren attended classes starting in 1789. The white-shuttered one-room building has been restored by the Redding Historical Society and is on the National Register of Historic Places.

28.5 Turn left onto Redding Road (CT 53).

Use caution on this busy stretch of road.

29.3 Turn right onto Limekiln Road.

Start a very steep 0.5-mile climb here.

31.1 Turn right onto Lonetown Road.

31.3 Turn left onto Putnam Park Road (CT 107).

32.1 Just before the junction of CT 58, you'll see the entrance to Putnam Memorial State Park on the left.

The entrance to this historic 230-acre park is graced by a bronze equestrian statue by renowned sculptor Anna Hyatt Huntington (see ride 22), depicting Gen. Israel Putnam's narrow escape in 1779 from British troops in Greenwich. The senior major general, known as "Old Put" by his loyal troops, led the right wing of Washington's Continental Army, which spent a bitter New England winter here during the Revolution. All that remains of the encampment are the walls and chimneys of the soldiers' huts, now reduced to rock piles. Reconstructed guard towers are also at the site.

32.2 *Bear left onto Black Rock Turnpike (CT 58).*

This turns into Redding Road as you cross the Bethel town line.

33.7 *Turn right onto Sunset Hill Road.*

33.8 *Take the first left onto Wolf-Pits Road.*

Enjoy the long, shady descent down this narrow road.

34.6 *Bear right at the Y-junction leading to Codfish Hill Road (unmarked). Turn right at the stop sign.*

35.8 *Turn left onto Codfish Hill Road Extenstion.*

36.2 *Make a sharp right turn onto Jacklin Road.*

Use caution descending this steep, narrow road.

36.5 *At the traffic light, turn right onto Sugar Street (CT 302).*

40.4 *At this traffic light, make a careful left turn through this busY-intersection onto Main Street (CT 25).*

41.0 *Turn left into the Edmond Town Hall parking lot to end the ride.*

Bicycle Shops

Bethel Cycle & Fitness, 120 Greenwood Avenue (CT 302), Bethel; 203-792-4640

Outdoor Sports Center, 80 Danbury Road (US 7), Wilton; 203-762-8797 or 1-800-782-2193

T C Cycle, 115 South Main Street (CT 25), Newtown; 203-426-9111

World of Bikes, 317 South Main Street (CT 25), Newtown; 203-426-3335

24
Chester to Killingworth

Distance: *39.3 miles*
Terrain: *Gradual to moderately rolling hills*
Difficulty: *Moderate*
Recommended bicycle: *Touring/road bike*

On this tour you'll ride through charming Connecticut River towns before heading west into the wooded rolling hills that most visitors to the Connecticut River Valley don't see.

Almost immediately you'll arrive in the upscale artists' community of Chester, bustling with galleries, bookstores, cafés, and shops. After that, the quaint towns of Deep River, Centerbrook, and Ivoryton are strung along this peaceful stretch of river, near the end of its 410-mile journey to Long Island Sound. Much of the lower river is undeveloped, thanks to the shifting sandbars that prevent the development of a deep-water harbor. With no port at its mouth, the river's wetlands are healthy and undisturbed, home to hundreds of species of wildlife.

Deep into the woods you'll pass miles of stone walls that follow tree-lined roads and disappear into forests, marking meadow boundaries abandoned long ago when woodlands once again claimed the land, mere remnants of the farms carved out of the rocky New England soil centuries ago.

The quiet river-valley town of Killingworth was home to a citizen who may not have been a household name, but whose work was treasured by many children growing up in the early 20th century. Hugh Lofting, creator of the famous children's stories about Dr. Dolittle, penned his stories from his home on Green Hill Road, near Evergreen Cemetery, where he is buried. When Lofting was a soldier in World War I, he wrote animated letters home to his children, and the Dr. Dolittle stories evolved from their correspondence.

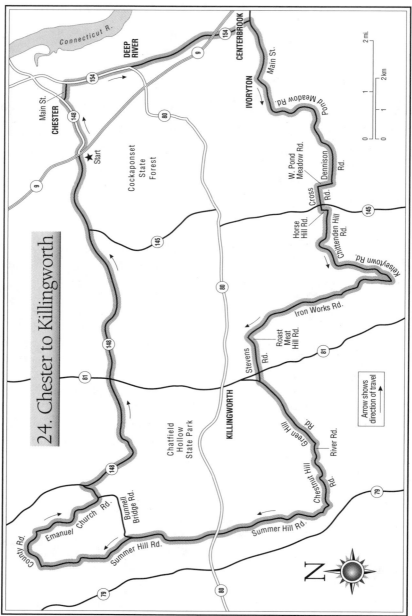

24. Chester to Killingworth

Connecticut R.

DEEP RIVER

CENTERBROOK

IVORYTON

Main St.

CHESTER
Main St.

★ Start

Cockaponset
State
Forest

Pond Meadow Rd.

W. Pond
Meadow Rd.
Cross
Rd.

Dennison
Rd.

Horse
Hill Rd.

Chittenden Hill
Rd.

Kelseytown Rd.

Iron Works Rd.

Roast
Meat
Hill Rd.

Stevens Rd.

KILLINGWORTH

Chatfield
Hollow
State Park

Green Hill
Rd.

River Rd.

Chestnut Hill
Rd.

Summer Hill Rd.

Bunnell
Bridge Rd.

Emanuel Church Rd.

County Rd.

Summer Hill Rd.

Arrow shows
direction of travel

N

2 mi.

2 km

Paul Woodward, © 2000 The Countryman Press

Directions for the Ride

The ride begins at the commuter parking lot at exit 6 off CT 9 in Chester. The lot is on the west side of the highway.

0.0 *Turn right out of the commuter parking lot onto CT 148 east.*

You'll pass under the highway and head east toward Chester. As you near the center of the village, you'll begin to see some lovely Colonial homes that were built for sea captains and wealthy merchants.

Just past the tiny Chester Library is the National Theatre of the Deaf, a highly acclaimed international touring company based in Chester.

1.4 *At the stop sign, turn right onto Main Street.*

The main avenue winding through this artsy town on the Pataconk River is almost always bustling with people walking the sidewalks and strolling in and out of cafés, galleries, and bookstores. This flurry of activity ends quickly as the road rises out of town toward the Connecticut River. Gristmills and sawmills flourished here in the 17th century, followed by a thriving shipbuilding industry.

1.9 *At the blinking traffic light, turn right onto CT 154 toward Deep River.*

This sleepy hamlet may not be as polished as Chester, but it has a quirky charm of its own that you'll notice as you ride along Main Street. Note the old factory (now turned into condos) called the Piano Works, where pianos were once made. This was also a big industry in Ivoryton; the town takes its name from ivory piano keys.

5.8 *At the traffic light in Centerbrook, turn right onto Main Street.*

7.2 *Follow Main Street as it heads left in the center of Ivoryton.*

Like its neighbor Deep River, this understated community has an off-the-beaten-path air. You'll feel you're the first to discover its offerings, like the romantic Copper Beech Inn, and the rustic brown-shingled Ivoryton Playhouse on the green, the country's oldest self-supporting summer theater. Across from the playhouse is the Ivoryton General Store, a good place to stop for a sandwich and a drink. People often relax on the steps out front.

7.9 Bear left onto Pond Meadow Road.

This road takes you into the northern fringes of Westbrook. Here you get a feel for what much of the ride will entail; winding, narrow wooded roads through quiet neighborhoods.

9.8 Bear right onto Dennison Road.

At the stop sign, turn right onto West Pond Meadow Road (unmarked).

10.8 Take the first left onto Cross Road.

11.2 Cross CT 145 and proceed straight onto Horse Hill Road. Shortly thereafter, go around a bend and turn right at the stop sign onto Chittenden Road.

As you crest this scenic road, the stone walls and old trees seem to squeeze it down to a narrow ribbon. On the hilltop is a unique wildlife rehabilitation and education center called Wind Over Wings (860-669-4904), specializing in the rehabilitation of coastal waterfowl and birds of prey. The center is open to the public by appointment only.

12.9 At the stop sign, turn left onto Kelseytown Road (unmarked).

14.1 Turn right onto Iron Works Road.

17.7 At the stop sign, turn left onto Roast Meat Hill Road.

17.9 Turn right onto Stevens Road.

18.4 At the stop sign, cross CT 81.

18.6 Turn left at this stop sign onto Green Hill Road.

Unlike the last few streets that were residential, this wooded road becomes very rural; you'll begin a long, gently rolling descent here.

19.4 At the stop sign, continue straight onto Green Hill Road.

20.4 Turn right onto River Road.

20.6 At the stop sign, proceed straight.

21.1 At the stop sign, bear right, following the sign for one-way traffic.

21.3 Turn left onto Chestnut Hill Road.

Cyclists can enjoy miles of peaceful back roads in the Connecticut River Valley.

This very narrow road winds downhill; near the bottom, cross a small bridge over the Hammonassett River.

22.0 *Turn right onto Summer Hill Road.*

24.5 *At the stop sign, cross CT 80.*

You'll leave civilization behind on this very pretty wooded road.

26.3 *At the Y-intersection, bear left (Bunnell Bridge Road is to the right).*

28.4 *At the stop sign, turn right onto County Road.*

Near the top of a rise, begin looking for a road to the right.

29.3 *Turn right onto Emanuel Church Road.*

It may seem odd that a rural road is named for a church, but as you descend through the forest you'll see a tidy white church at the end of a dirt road. The Emanuel Episcopal Church of Killingworth was built in 1800. Check out the tower bell (next to the church) and the intricately paned windows.

31.4 *At the stop sign, turn right onto CT 148 and follow it east toward Chester.*

On this main road the hills are longer and steeper than the tight, narrow bends of the side roads. In about 5 miles, you'll cross into Chester. Straddling the town line is the Inn at Chester (860-526-9541), a 1776 farmhouse converted into an elegant country inn and restaurant.

39.3 Just before the junction of CT 9, turn right into the commuter parking lot to end the ride.

Bicycle Shops

Clarke Cycles, Essex Plaza (CT 154), Essex; 860-767-2405

Cycles of Madison, 698 Boston Post Road (US 1), Madison; 203-245-8735 or 1-800-245-TREK

Pedal Power Cycle & Fitness, 500 Main Street, Middletown; 860-347-3776

Saybrook Cycle Works, 210 Main Street, Old Saybrook; 860-388-1534

Cockaponset State Forest

Distance: *10 miles of roads; 20 miles of trails*
Terrain: *Rolling dirt forest roads and rugged singletrack trails*
Difficulty: *Moderate*
Recommended bicycle: *Mountain bike*

This 15,652-acre state forest, Connecticut's second largest, spreads itself across the rural Connecticut River Valley towns of Chester and Haddam. It's named for Chief Cockaponset, a Native American sachem.

The forest is laced with about 20 miles of doubletrack and technical singletrack trails that follow rocky ridgelines and crisscross the forest roads; you can ride for hours by connecting these various paths. The wide forest roads climb and descend these ridges somewhat gradually, while the side trails have shorter, steeper dips and drops. Many are covered with rocks, exposed roots, and various obstructions.

Mountain bikes are prohibited from some trails—like the blue-blazed Cockaponset Trail—which are posted with FOOT TRAIL ONLY signs. Please respect these closures.

This sprawling forest includes a wide variety of terrain. Rock outcroppings and ledges are connected by rolling hills drained by streams flowing toward the Pattaconk Reservoir. Brushy ponds and marshes surrounded by azaleas and other dense shrubbery complete the landscape. Around the forest you'll see stands of red spruce, pine, and hemlock, and in June, a profusion of mountain laurel drapes the hills with its cloudy pink blossoms. The rest of the year the bushes are thick with clusters of dark green leaves.

Many of the side trails, dams, and stone ditches are the work of the Civilian Conservation Corps. Through the presence of the CCC—the federal program that provided jobs during the Depression—there were

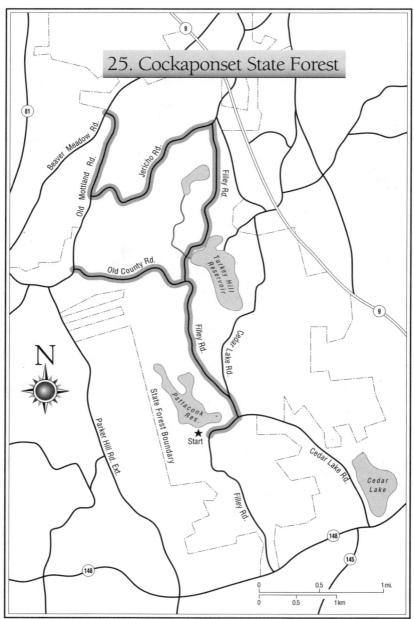

25. Cockaponset State Forest

more forest workers in Cockaponset in the 1930s than the state of Connecticut currently has in its entire system of more than 100 state parks and forests.

You can picnic, sunbathe, and swim at the Pattaconk Reservoir, also known as Russell Jennings Pond. This popular spot is also the beginning of the ride.

For trail maps and other information, call the forest headquarters (860-345-8521) or write Cockaponset State Forest, Ranger Road, Haddam, CT 06438.

Directions for the Ride

Take CT 9 to exit 6 in Chester. Follow West Main Street (CT 148) west toward Killingworth. In about 1.5 miles you'll pass Cedar Lake and Camp Hazen (YMCA). Immediately after the lake turn right onto Cedar Lake Road; you'll see a brown sign here designating Pattaconk Lake State Recreation Area. Follow Cedar Lake Road for about 1.5 miles and turn left at the sign for Pattaconk Lake. There is ample parking on both sides of the forest road past the reservoir.

About the Ride

Touring the forest roads will mean lots of moderate, steady climbing combined with descents ranging from gentle to plunging. Many of these scenic dirt roads climb to wooded hilltops before dropping down to marshes and ponds at lower elevations. Unfortunately, the layout of these roads is not conducive to planning a loop; they are meant more for exploration, which will entail some backtracking. Riding here is nonetheless fun and rewarding.

From Pattaconk Reservoir, you can take the unmarked paved road (Filley Road) that descends for about 0.5 mile toward Cedar Lake Road. At that junction, turn left onto Cedar Lake Road, then take another left to rejoin Filley Road (look for the brown state forest sign). This paved road heads north into the forest, and from it you'll see many well-worn side trails spreading into the woods.

If you don't take the trails, you can follow Filley Road as it climbs gradually and its surface turns to gravel. Just past a group of youth campsites, the road begins a winding descent, crosses into the town of Haddam, and eventually comes to a junction with Old County Road, an unpaved forest road on the left. This intersection is about 2 miles from the Pattaconk Reservoir.

You can take Old County Road to the left to see Hackney Marsh, a particularly lovely pond whose surface is covered with a profusion of large water-lily blossoms.

If you continue straight on Filley Road, you'll descend deeper into the forest and shortly arrive at scenic Turkey Hill Reservoir. At this point, the road is blocked by a cement barricade; ride around it and follow Filley Road as it crests another wooded hill and drops quickly down the other side.

Near the bottom of the descent, you can turn left at the Y-intersection onto Jericho Road, a marked dirt forest road. This road rolls up and down a couple of short hills before beginning a long, fairly challenging sustained climb. At the top, the road bends abruptly to the right, then twists steeply downhill to paved Beaver Meadow Road. At this junction, you are roughly 4 miles from Turkey Hill Reservoir and 6 miles from the start of the ride.

Many trails fan off Jericho Road; you may decide to leave the road and explore some of these more rugged paths, some which connect to Old County Road. Your other option is to backtrack on the forest roads.

Bicycle Shops

Clarke Cycles, Essex Plaza (CT 154), Essex; 860-767-2405

Pedal Power Cycle & Fitness, 500 Main Street, Middletown; 860-347-3776

26

Connecticut River Crossings:
Essex to East Haddam

Distance: *40.5 miles (about 25 miles, omitting the Devil's Hopyard section)*
Terrain: *Flat stretches with rolling to moderately challenging hills*
Difficulty: *Strenuous*
Recommended bicycle: *Touring/road bike*

It's difficult to pick a favorite highlight on this tour because it has so much to offer. A trip through Essex, an 18th-century maritime village considered the country's best small town, according to *The 100 Best Small Towns in America*. A river crossing on a ferry service in operation on the Connecticut River since 1769, with Gillette Castle reigning from a high bluff. A road hugging the shore of the beautiful Connecticut River, whose tidal creeks and salt marshes have been designated by the Nature Conservancy as one of the hemisphere's 40 "Last Great Places." Or riding by the Goodspeed, an ornate Victorian opera house, and crossing the river on an antique swing bridge.

That isn't everything. There's the cool, dark forest and cascading waterfall in Devil's Hopyard State Park and the peaceful, unhurried atmosphere of the country lanes and hill towns in between.

The first stop is the village of Essex, whose handsome white clapboard Colonial and Federal houses have been lovingly preserved. At the end of Main Street, the town's 1878 dock house where steamboats used to stop is now the Connecticut River Museum, which depicts the area's seafaring heritage and the natural and human history of the river valley.

A centuries-old ferry operation still shuttles people across the Connecticut River from Chester to Hadlyme at the unhurried pace of long ago. The first ferry was propelled by ferrymen with long wooden poles;

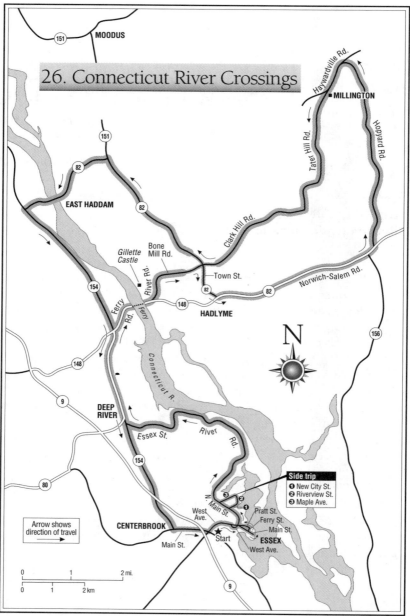

26. Connecticut River Crossings

151
MOODUS

Haywardville Rd.
■ MILLINGTON

151

Tater Hill Rd.

82

Hopyard Rd.

EAST HADDAM

82

Clark Hill Rd.

Bone
Mill Rd.

Gillette
Castle

River Rd.

Town St.

Norwich-Salem Rd.

154

Ferry Rd.

Ferry

82

82

148

HADLYME

N

148

156

9

Connecticut R.

DEEP
RIVER

Essex St.

River Rd.

80

154

Side trip
❶ New City St.
❷ Riverview St.
❸ Maple Ave.

❸

❷

❶

Arrow shows
direction of travel

CENTERBROOK

West
Ave.

N. Main St.

Pratt St.
Ferry St.
Main St.

ESSEX

Start

Main St.

West Ave.

0   1   2 mi.
0   1   2 km

9

today's boat, the steel-hulled *Selden III,* is powered by diesel engines. Passengers in the 18th century paid threepence to go across with a horse. The prices have risen, but there is still no greater bargain for 3 minutes of one of the most sublime rides you'll experience.

After crossing the river you'll take a winding forest road through Devil's Hopyard. History is rife with legends and folklore alluding to the origin of the park's name and the presence of mysterious potholes at the base of thundering Chapman Falls.

One account has Satan sitting on a boulder at the top of the 60-foot cascade while the Black Witches of Haddam cavorted in the circular potholes formed in the rocks at the bottom of the falls.

Local speculation also points to the possibility that the word *Devil* in the park's name evolved from the name Dibble, a local farmer and bootlegger who had a hopyard near the falls. Another folk legend claims the potholes are the work of the Devil's hooves, from hopping ledge to ledge to avoid the falls.

The last stop on this tour is the village of East Haddam, whose gleaming white, six-story Goodspeed Opera House presides over the Connecticut River like a colossal wedding cake, a shrine to a colorful era when steamers brought theatergoers from New York to see nationally acclaimed productions. Revivals and new musicals are still staged there.

Directions for the Ride

Start the ride in Essex at the commuter parking lot on CT 154 at exit 3 off CT 9 (around the corner from the Essex Steam Train). You'll pass small food stores all along the route; Clarke Cycles is on CT 154, right around the corner from the commuter lot in Essex Plaza, in case you need any supplies.

0.0 *From the parking lot, turn right onto Saybrook Road (CT 154).*

Make an immediate right onto West Avenue.

0.6 *Turn right onto Chaplin Square.*

This is unmarked, but you will see a sign pointing to Essex village.

0.8 *Turn right onto Main Street.*

Use caution riding down this congested one-way road through the heart of Essex. In addition to its plethora of shops, Main Street has a range of eateries, from delis to an inn and tavern dating to the Revolution. The rambling white Griswold Inn ("The Griz") is a local landmark, famous for its traditional Yankee fare and live jazz.

In the 18th and 19th centuries, Essex was one of state's most important shipbuilding centers; a British raid during the War of 1812 burned 28 ships. The first U.S. warship, the *Oliver Cromwell,* was launched from the village before the War of Independence.

1.3 Take the first right onto Ferry Street.

Follow the road as it curves left at the boatyards. You'll go down a street with architecture as beautiful as that on Main Street, but without the traffic and crowds.

1.5 Go straight through one stop sign, then turn right onto North Main Street at the next one.

Side Trip: To see some fine examples of restored sea captains' homes, turn right onto New City Street, bear left on Riverview Street, go left on Maple Avenue, then turn right on North Main Street to rejoin the main loop.

North Main Street turns into River Road as it crosses into Deep River. The tidal creeks and salt marshes here are home to ospreys and bald eagles; the handsome estates strung along the broad Connecticut River reflect the prosperity of the area's seafaring past.

6.0 Bear right onto Essex Street.

7.0 At the stop sign, turn right onto Main Street (CT 154) into Deep River.

Side Trip: Turn left onto Main Street (look for a sign pointing to the Chester business district) to visit the eclectic village of Chester.

9.1 At the traffic light, turn right onto Ferry Road (CT 148) to the Chester/Hadlyme ferry slip on the west bank of the Connecticut River.

Continue north on CT 154.

Although the ferry has been outmoded by bridges, many tourists and commuters still find its history and charm a welcome sojourn from the bustle of modern life.

Ospreys, egrets, and eagles are among the wildlife you may see during the river crossing, but a sight you definitely won't miss is

The Chester-Hadlyme ferry has crossed the Connecticut River since 1769.

the medievallike fortress perched on a towering bluff in the chain of hills known as the Seven Sisters. It is a majestic homage to the eccentricities of actor and playwright William Gillette, best known for his portrayal of Sherlock Holmes. Gillette built the 24-room fieldstone mansion in 1919; it served as his retirement home until his death in 1937. The castle and grounds are now a state park.

10.0 *Disembark the ferry and bear left at the first stop sign onto River Road (look for the brown sign pointing to Gillette Castle).*

10.6 *Turn right onto Bone Mill Road.*

11.5 *At the Y-intersection, bear right to continue on Bone Mill Road (unmarked).*

11.7 At the stop sign, turn right onto Town Street (CT 82).

12.4 At the next stop sign, continue on CT 82 as it turns left and becomes Norwich-Salem Road.

The Hadlyme Country Store on the right is a good stop for food or supplies. This crossroads, known locally as Hadlyme Four Corners, gets its name from the nearby towns of Haddam and Lyme.

15.9 Turn left onto Hopyard Road (look for the brown sign for Devil's Hopyard State Park, just past the junction of CT 156).

This scenic road winds, curves, and dips all the way through the park and, combined with the absence of a shoulder, requires much caution.

The cornerstone of this 860-acre park is Chapman Falls, whose waters tumble over 60 feet of rocky falls. About 3 miles up Hopyard Road, past the main entrance to the park, look for a brown sign indicating the campground and falls area.

20.2 At the stop sign, turn left onto Haywardville Road.

The dense woods of Devil's Hopyard give way here to beautiful meadows enclosed by old stone walls and historic homesteads.

21.0 At the hilltop village of Millington, turn left onto Tater Hill Road.

This tiny green is fronted by only three antique homes. A couple of miles down the road you'll pass Tater Hill Burying Ground, a cluster of worn headstones surrounded by stone walls.

25.0 Bear right onto Clark Hill Road (Mill Road goes to the right here).

26.5 At the stop sign, turn right onto CT 82 and follow it into East Haddam.

This is a very hilly section, mostly descending into the village.

In town, you'll see the 1736 Gelston House, now an inn and restaurant, and the 1876 opera house, built by affluent shipbuilder and merchant William Goodspeed. You'll pedal out of town on a 1913 swing bridge—locally known as "the Singing Bridge" because of the sound cars make as they cross its metal grate—believed to be the longest such bridge in the world. It frequently swings open to allow boats to pass underneath.

31.9 At the traffic light, turn left on CT 154/CT 82.
Follow CT 154 into Centerbrook.

39.7 At the traffic light in Centerbrook, follow CT 154 to the left toward the junction of CT 9.

40.5 Turn left into the commuter parking lot to end the tour.

Ferry Information

Fare for bike and rider: $1.50

Hours: April 1 through November 30, Monday through Friday, 7–6:45; Saturday and Sunday, 10:30–5.

Bicycle Shops

Clarke Cycles, Essex Plaza (CT 154), Essex; 860-767-2405

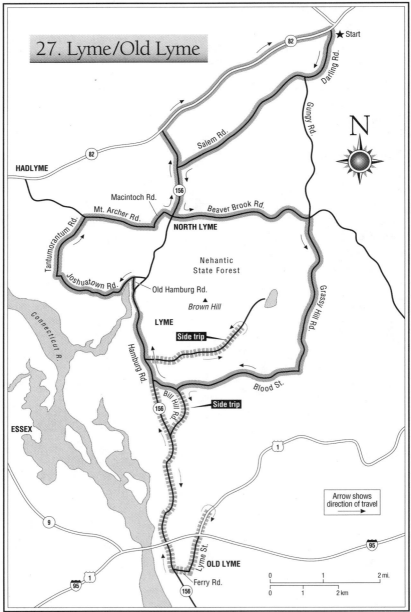

27. Lyme/Old Lyme

★ Start

Darling Rd.

Gungy Rd.

82

Salem Rd.

HADLYME

82

156

Macintoch Rd.

Mt. Archer Rd.

Tantumorantum Rd.

Beaver Brook Rd.

NORTH LYME

Joshuatown Rd.

Old Hamburg Rd.

Nehantic
State Forest

Brown Hill

LYME

Side trip

Hamburg Rd.

Connecticut R.

Grassy Hill Rd.

Side trip

Blood St.

ESSEX

156

Bill Hill Rd.

Side trip

1

Arrow shows
direction of travel

9

95

Lyme St.

OLD LYME

1

95

Ferry Rd.

156

N

| 0 | | 1 | | 2 mi. |
| 0 | 1 | | 2 km | |

27
Lyme/Old Lyme

Distance: *27 miles (37 miles with side trips to Old Lyme and Uncas Lake)*
Terrain: *Flat with some low hills and two moderately steep climbs*
Difficulty: *Moderate to strenuous*
Recommended bicycle: *Touring/road bike*

This route was seemingly made for cyclists. Its rural landscape of orchards, dairy farms, stone walls, and antique homes lend it an unhurried atmosphere as you pedal through peaceful little backwater hamlets like North Lyme and Hamburg Cove. Often gems like these are tucked high in the hills, which for a cyclist means a lot of climbing. Here, however, the hills are gentle, and aside from a couple of challenging climbs, the ride is fairly moderate.

Hamburg Cove is considered one of the prettiest spots in Connecticut. This quiet community of historic clapboard homes sits at the confluence of the Eight Mile and Connecticut Rivers. The road rising above the narrow, 3-mile cove offers a sublime view of boats moored in the shimmering water. Pedaling alongside a rambling clapboard home perched on a hill high above Hamburg, it's easy to imagine the wife of a sea captain pacing the widow's walk, watching the cove below for a familiar ship to come into sight.

You can extend the route by taking a side trip into Old Lyme, just a few miles south of the main loop on CT 156. This stately village at the mouth of the Connecticut River was a shipbuilding and trading center as well as home to the Lyme Art Colony, the hub of the American Impressionist movement. Some of the country's most famous Impressionist artists, Henry Ward Ranger and Childe Hassam among them, painted the landscape here and stayed in Florence Griswold's boardinghouse on Lyme Street. Today the 1817 Federal mansion at 96 Lyme Street is the

Florence Griswold Museum and the village's chief tourist attraction. The Lyme Art Association at 90 Lyme Street is the oldest summer art colony and gallery in the United States.

The next side trip, just a few miles north on CT 156, is to Uncas Lake, accessed by a dirt road through the thick woods of Nehantic State Forest. There is a small beach and picnic area on the lakeshore.

Directions for the Ride

Start at Salem Valley Farms Ice Cream on Darling Road in Salem, near the junction of CT 82 and CT 11. Enter the parking area and go to the far end of the dirt lot, away from the building. Salem Valley Farms is revered by locals and tourists alike who crowd this converted red barn for its rich, creamy homemade ice cream—a good way to end a ride.

0.0 From the parking lot, turn left onto Darling Road.

This quiet back road typifies most of this route by scenic river-valley farms and rural country estates.

0.2 At the stop sign, continue on Darling Road by heading straight across this four-way intersection.

1.3 Turn left at this stop sign to continue on Darling Road.

This very peaceful country road turns into Salem Road as you cross the Lyme town line.

4.3 At the stop sign, turn left onto Hamburg Road (CT 156).

From this junction, descend into the tiny village of Lyme.

5.3 Just past Lyme Consolidated School, turn left onto Beaver Brook Road.

8.0 Turn right onto Grassy Hill Road at this stop sign.

A beautifully restored Colonial homestead surrounded by woods and stone walls sits at the crest of this fairly steep, mile-long climb.

Just down the road is the quaint, classic Grassy Hill Congregational Church. Founded in 1746, it now holds services only during the summer.

11.2 Turn right onto Blood Street.

This winding road follows the north shore of Rogers Lake and includes one moderate climb.

Summer services are still held at the 1746 Grassy Hill Congregational Church.

13.7 **Blood Street forks at the end; bear right onto Bill Hill Road.**

Side Trip: To ride to Old Lyme, bear left at the fork onto Bill Hill Road, turn left onto Neck Road (CT 156), and follow this road for about 3 miles; you'll cross I-95/US 1. Turn left onto Ferry Road and then take another left onto Lyme Street. Follow CT 156 north to return to the main route.

14.3 **At the stop sign, turn right onto Hamburg Road (CT 156).**

Side Trip to Uncas Lake (approximately 2 miles, one-way): About 0.5 mile up CT 156 you'll see a brown sign for Nehantic State Forest; turn right on this forest road that alternates between unimproved pavement and dirt (you can manage it on a road bike). Bear left at the first junction, then follow signs to the Uncas Lake beach and picnic area.

In the 17th century, Chief Uncas was the grand sachem of the Mohegans, a tribe that at one time occupied much of southern Connecticut. He was the model for James Fenimore Cooper's novel *The Last of the Mohicans*. Uncas's grave is in an ancient burial ground at Fort Shantok State Park in Uncasville.

15.7 **Pass through the colonial village of Hamburg.**

This roadside cluster of picket fences and Colonial buildings includes the 1859 H. L. Reynolds Co. General Store, where you can pick up food and drinks.

16.0 **Bear left onto Old Hamburg Road.**

This road will take you along the edge of the picturesque Hamburg Cove.

16.2 **At the stop sign, turn left onto Joshuatown Road (unmarked).**

This road circles the cove before rising above it.

18.1 **At the bottom of the hill, turn right onto Tantumorantum Road.**

Ride along rock-strewn Rams Horn Creek.

19.4 **At the end of Tantumorantum Road, turn right onto Mount Archer Road (the sign reads BUSH HILL ROAD, which goes to the left).**

This fairly steep climb will take you to the top of Mount Archer, an undeveloped wooded hilltop managed by the Lyme Land Trust. Use caution when making the fast descent down the other side.

20.8 *After descending Mount Archer Road, bear left onto Macintosh Road.*

21.3 *At the stop sign, turn left onto Hamburg Road (CT 156).*

You'll pass through the village of Lyme and enter East Haddam just after crossing the Eight Mile River.

23.1 *Turn right onto Norwich-Salem Road (CT 82) at the end of CT 156.*

This road has many flat sections linked by a few gentle hills. It can be a heavily trafficked route on weekends.

26.9 *Turn right onto Darling Road, then shortly make a left into the Salem Valley Farms parking lot to end the ride.*

Bicycle Shops

The Bicycle Post, 310 Flanders Road (CT 161), East Lyme; 860-739-6181

Clarke Cycles, Essex Plaza (CT 154), Essex; 860-767-2405

THE SHORELINE: GREENWICH TO STONINGTON

28

Greenwich: The Backcountry

Distance: *21.9 miles*
Terrain: *Rolling hills with several steep climbs and descents*
Difficulty: *Strenuous*
Recommended bicycle: *Touring/road bike*

One can argue that Fairfield County has closer ties to New York City than New England. Due to this relationship, the extreme southwest corner of Connecticut has been dubbed the "Gold Coast," referring to its proximity to Manhattan and its fast-paced, sophisticated culture.

Many travelers in search of quintessential New England dismiss Greenwich as a bedroom community for those who make their fortunes in Manhattan and come home to the opulent estates and palatial mansions tucked behind imposing gates. However, you'll notice glimpses of New England character while riding through the rolling hills and northern reaches of Greenwich, known as "the Backcountry." Scattered along many of these winding country lanes are more modest but equally charming Colonial homes set behind ancient trees and stone walls.

This gentrified town has indeed come a long way since it was settled in 1640 by two Englishmen who purchased the land from local Native Americans for 25 coats. But despite its gilded image, relatively quiet, scenic roads can be found, as well as 18th-century farmhouses, stately English manors, Mediterranean-style villas, and Georgian mansions. This is quiet countryside, a green landscape dotted with horse farms, polo fields, and acres of woodlands protected by the Audubon Society.

Connecticut's first art colony—attracting such famous American Impressionists as J. Alden Weir, Childe Hassam, and John Henry Twachtman—was in the Cos Cob section of town. Their landscapes are what many consider classic New England—meadows, stone walls, white

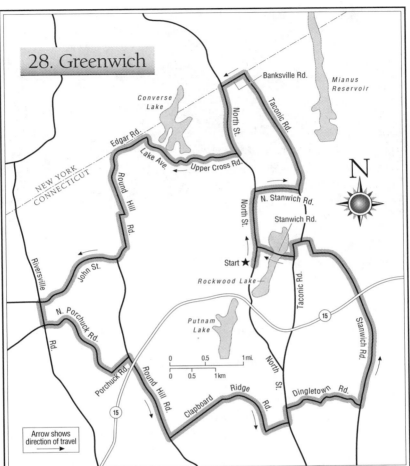

28. Greenwich

Banksville Rd.

Mianus Reservoir

Converse Lake

North St.

Taconic Rd.

Edgar Rd.

Lake Ave.

Upper Cross Rd.

NEW YORK
CONNECTICUT

Round Hill Rd.

North St.

N. Stanwich Rd.

Stanwich Rd.

N

Riversville Rd.

John St.

Start ★

Rockwood Lake

Taconic Rd.

N. Porchuck Rd.

Rd.

Putnam Lake

15

Stanwich Rd.

Porchuck Rd.

Round Hill Rd.

0   0.5   1 mi.
0   0.5   1 km

North St.

Clapboard Ridge Rd.

Dingletown Rd.

15

Arrow shows
direction of travel

Paul Woodward, © 2000 The Countryman Press

church spires. Greenwich had the combination of light, color, and subject matter that inspired these artists, whose style was unprecedented.

Directions for the Ride

Start at the dirt parking area of the Babcock Preserve on North Street, about 0.5 mile north of exit 31 off the Merritt Parkway. Look for a brown sign and stone gateposts designating the entrance.

A spot for quiet reflection in Greenwich's Audubon Fairchild Wildflower Garden.

0.0 *Turn left out of the parking area onto North Street.*

This is a busy road during rush hour, thanks to its proximity to the Merritt Parkway. The terrain starts out flat but quickly begins rising past lavish gated estates, imparting an immediate sense of this community's affluence.

1.1 *Turn right onto North Stanwich Road.*

You will see a white wooden sign for Stanwich Congregational Church pointing down this quiet, tree-lined street.

1.7 *North Stanwich Road dips to a stop sign; turn left here onto Taconic Road.*

A 1-mile climb begins here, which is initially steep and then tapers to a more gradual ascent. At the top of the hill are the rolling meadows and white fences of two sizable farms, Lionshare and White Birch. Like much of Greenwich, many of the side roads are private.

3.7 *Follow Taconic Road as it turns sharply to the left, becoming Banksville Road.*

You'll immediately see a sign for Banksville, which straddles the Connecticut/New York border. This is a quiet neighborhood of neat, modest homes. About 0.2 mile down the road is the Banksville Deli & Bakery.

4.1 At the stop sign, turn left onto North Street.

The plaza on the right has a small grocery store and a pizza restaurant.

5.1 Turn right onto Upper Cross Road.

You will climb a short rise before making a winding, narrow descent.

6.1 At the next stop sign, bear right onto Lake Avenue.

This road skirts Converse Lake, not visible from the route, on the Connecticut/New York border. The road is very narrow and winding with several short, steep climbs and descents.

6.8 Bear left onto Edgar Road.

7.3 At the stop sign, turn left onto Round Hill Road.

9.2 Turn right onto John Street.

The stark, white First Church of Round Hill, founded in 1810, is on the corner here. Begin a 1-mile steep descent before starting the short, strenuous climb to North Greenwich.

10.6 At the stop sign, turn left onto Riversville Road.

The Audubon Center, established here in 1941, is through the white gates on the right at the stop sign. The 485-acre sanctuary and nature store are open daily 9–5. There is a hawk-watch area, interpretive programs, and hiking trails at this beautiful hillside preserve.

As you turn onto Riversville Road, watch for the North Greenwich Congregational Church, on this corner since the mid-1800s. Many of the town's earliest families and settlers have been laid to rest in its tiny cemetery.

10.9 Turn left onto North Porchuk Road.

About 0.5 mile down a steep descent on the right is the Audubon Fairchild Wildflower Garden (look for a green sign and gate). This peaceful 134-acre sanctuary is laced with trails that pass ponds, meadows, streams, a mature oak-beech-maple forest, and rocky ravines—all home to a diverse array of flowers, birds, and other wildlife. Visitors to this gem of a site should be grateful to a 19th-century nature lover. Benjamin Fairchild toiled for 40 years at this site to preserve the fields and woodlands. The result is a natural garden with wildflowers, trees, ferns, and other plants native to Connecticut. His simple vision was to preserve the "small things we tread on and do not see" for future generations of visitors. Fairchild's nephew donated the land to the Audubon Society in 1945. Bikes are not allowed on the trails; you can lock your bike at the green gate near the information kiosk and explore the trails on foot.

12.1 *Bear left at the Y-intersection, then immediately left at the stop sign to continue on North Porchuck Road.*

12.7 *At the stop sign, make a right turn onto Round Hill Road.*

This road will cross over the Merritt Parkway; use caution near the entrance ramps in this busy area.

14.0 *With the Round Hill Country Club on your right, turn left onto Clapboard Ridge Road.*

Descend this mile-long steep hill all the way to the next stop sign.

15.0 *At this stop sign, turn right onto Lake Avenue, then immediately turn left to continue on Clapboard Ridge Road.*

You will climb a short, steep hill here before descending again.

16.0 *Turn left at the next stop sign. This is still Clapboard Ridge Road.*

16.3 *At this stop sign, turn left onto North Street (unmarked). You'll stay on North Street only for a short time.*

16.5 *Turn right onto Dingletown Road.*

17.8 *Turn left onto Stanwich Road.*

You'll pass the tiny Dingletown Community Church on the left, a quaint black-shuttered nondenominational chapel built in 1845.

19.1 *At this sharp curve, follow Stanwich Road to the left (Guinea Road is to the right).*

In a short while, you will again cross over the Merritt Parkway.

20.8 *At the Y-intersection, bear left toward a stop sign. Proceed straight onto Taconic Road.*

21.1 *Turn left onto South Stanwich Road.*

At the base of a steep descent is a one-lane causeway cutting between scenic Putnam and Rockwood Lakes.

21.6 *At the stop sign, turn left onto North Street, following the sign for the Merritt Parkway.*

21.9 *Turn right into the Babcock Preserve parking area to end the ride.*

Bicycle Shops

Buzz's Cycles, 1 Boulder Avenue, Old Greenwich; 203-637-1665

Dave's Cycle and Fitness, 78 Valley Road, Cos Cob; 203-661-7736 or 203-661-7803

Don's Cycle Shop, 1964 Post Road (US 1), Fairfield; 203-255-4079

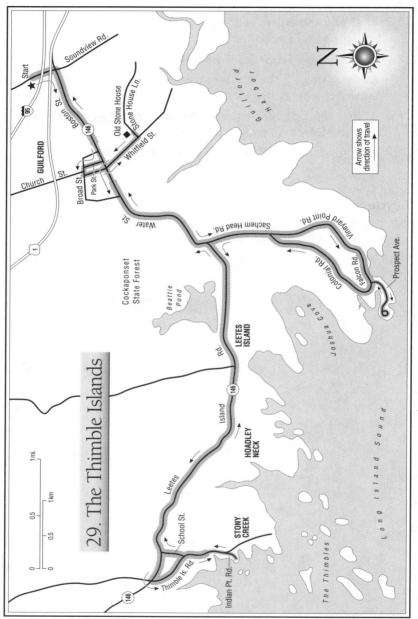

29. The Thimble Islands

29
The Thimble Islands

Distance: 19.1 miles
Terrain: Flat
Difficulty: Easy
Recommended bicycle: Touring/road bike

Guilford's village green, laid out in 1639, is as classic as any in New England—a lovingly landscaped common presided over by Colonial homes and several churches, the most noteworthy being the 19th-century Greek Revival Congregational church. Around town, there are 400 18th- and 19th-century buildings.

Harriet Beecher Stowe lived on her grandmother's Guilford farm when she was four. Some speculate that seeing the family's indentured servants could have been the earliest inspiration for her seminal novel, *Uncle Tom's Cabin.*

The highlight of this pleasant shoreline tour—aside from the sweet tang of salt air—is the picture-perfect seaside village of Stony Creek and the sprinkling of tiny islets just off the coast, known collectively as the Thimble Islands. Together they form an enclave of seclusion and peace that only living on a private island can bring, enjoyed by those who savor isolation and can afford to buy it.

About 25 of the islands are inhabited. Some are little more than granite outcroppings with room for only one cottage; others, like Money Island, are home to a handful of houses. Many do without electricity and phones, and some residents even pump their own water.

Island architecture runs the gamut, from Newport-style mansions with seaside gardens and landscaped swimming pools to simpler but equally charming Victorian-era cottages with wraparound porches adorned with rocking chairs and hammocks. These summer homes, many built by wealthy industrialists, are as overwhelmingly beautiful as their 360-degree views of the sea.

Directions for the Ride

This tour begins in Guilford at the commuter parking lot on Goose Lane, just off CT 146. It can be reached by taking exit 59 off I-95, or by taking Boston Post Road (US 1) into Guilford from the east or west.

0.0 *Turn right out of the parking lot onto Goose Lane.*

0.1 *At the traffic light, go straight across Boston Post Road (US 1).*

0.2 *Turn right onto Boston Street (CT 146).*

Among the historic homes lining the way to the Guilford green are the Thomas Hyland House, a 1660 red saltbox, and the Thomas Griswold House, a Colonial saltbox complete with blacksmith shop and historic herb garden, where five generations of the Griswold family lived.

1.2 *At the stop sign, you'll be at the corner of the Guilford green. Turn right onto Park Street to follow the east side of this tree-lined common.*

Cute boutiques, mom-and-pop convenience stores, and the Guilford Library are all found here.

1.4 *Turn left at the stop sign onto Broad Street.*

1.5 *Turn left onto Whitfield Street.*

1.9 *Bear left onto Old Whitfield Street.*

2.1 *Turn left onto Stone House Lane to reach the Henry Whitfield State Museum.*

This imposing 1639 stone house is the oldest in Connecticut and is New England's oldest stone building. The Reverend Henry Whitfield was the minister and leader of Guilford's first settlers. The house was opened in 1899 as the state's first museum.

From here, retrace your route up Whitfield Street to the green.

2.6 *At the stop sign, turn left onto Water Street (CT 146).*

3.9 *Turn right to continue on CT 146, which is now Leetes Island Road.*

This scenic shoreline road passes the expansive salt marshes that fringe Long Island Sound all the way to Stony Creek.

7.6 At the stop sign, turn left onto Thimble Island Road.

Just past the Stony Creek General Store is the Puppet House Theatre (203-488-5752). This rustic and casual community theater is also a puppet museum, featuring lifelike turn-of-the-20th-century Sicilian puppets.

8.2 Arrive at the center of Stony Creek.

Victorian cottages, shops, and cafés overlook the Thimble Islands and the bustling water traffic of fishing boats, kayakers (a couple of outfitters are based in the village), sailboats, and ferries. The narrow streets can get clogged with traffic and pedestrians, so use caution when pedaling through town.

Those not fortunate enough to call the islands their summer home can cruise around them by boat. Several tour companies leave from the Stony Creek Dock, taking passengers around some of the as many as 365 islands (depending on who's counting, and what people consider an actual island). Your captain will surely spin yarns about island folklore, such as the legendary exploits of Capt. William Kidd, who plied these waters and stashed some treasure on one of the islands in 1699. You may also hear stories of Tom Thumb, who was enamored with an island resident and likewise became one of the archipelago's more famous guests. Cut-in-Two Island, Mother-in-Law Island, and Beers Island also have their stories.

8.4 Leave Stony Creek by taking School Street back to CT 146, then head back toward Guilford.

11.7 At the stop sign, turn right onto Sachem Head Road.

This peninsula of summer cottages is named for a bloody battle that took place here in 1637 during the Pequot War. The Mohegans, led by Chief Uncas, captured a small band of Pequots that sought refuge on the narrow point of land. By some accounts, Uncas displayed the head of a Pequot sachem in an oak tree.

12.4 At the stop sign, bear left onto Vineyard Point Road.

13.3 Bear right at this unmarked Y-intersection.

13.7 Turn left onto Prospect Avenue.

14.1 Turn left onto Chimney Circle.

14.7 Turn left onto Falcon Road.

14.8 Turn right onto Colonial Road.

15.9 At the stop sign, turn left onto Sachem Head Road.

16.5 At the next stop sign, go straight onto Water Street (CT 146).

17.8 At this stop sign, turn left and then take an immediate right.
Follow the southern edge of the Guilford green as CT 146 turns into Boston Street.

18.9 At the blinking red light, turn left onto Goose Lane.

19.1 The ride ends at the commuter parking lot.

Bicycle Shops

Cycles of Madison, 698 Boston Post Road (US 1), Madison; 203-245-8735 or 1-800-245-TREK

Pete's Cycles and Stoves, 934 Boston Post Road (US 1), Guilford; 203-453-3544

Zane's Cycles, 105 North Main Street (US 1), Branford; 1-800-551-2453

30
Old Saybrook: Shore Points

Distance: *8.9 miles*
Terrain: *Flat*
Difficulty: *Easy*
Recommended bicycle: *Touring/road bike*

Saybrook was settled in the 1630s by an English company of colonists, making it one of Connecticut's oldest communities. A fort was built at the mouth of the Connecticut River to protect the new colony, whose ideal location, bordered on two sides by the river and Long Island Sound, made it a bustling center for maritime trade. (Saybrook Point was the former site of a trading post established earlier in the 17th century by the Dutch West Indies Company.) The settlement was later divided into the smaller river and shoreline communities of Old Saybrook, Chester, Deep River, Essex, Lyme, Old Lyme, and Westbrook.

This colonial shoreline community was the hometown of David Bushnell, inventor of the first submarine, the American Turtle. It was tested in the waters off Otter Cove in Essex, with Benjamin Franklin among those in attendance. Despite the military significance of Bushnell's invention, Old Saybrook today is better known as the home of actress Katharine Hepburn.

Yale College was founded here in 1701. School officials felt Old Saybrook was too isolated, however, and amid angry protests from residents, they relocated the college to New Haven.

As you ride past the numerous coves and marshes on this pleasant route, you might see some of the herons and egrets that thrive in this shoreline habitat. Along the quiet streets off North Cove are grand homes built by wealthy merchants and sea captains. More than 100 of Old Saybrook's homes are designated for their historical significance, mostly

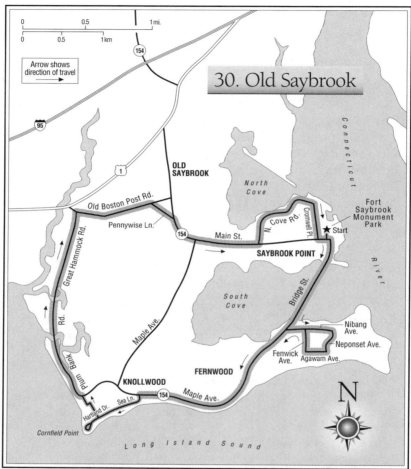

18th-century Colonial and 19th-century Federal homes, as well as a few 17th-century saltboxes and Georgian buildings.

Directions for the Ride

Start at Fort Saybrook Monument Park, on CT 154 at Saybrook Point. The small park is on the site of a fort built in 1635 that was destroyed by fire in 1647.

0.0 *At the park entrance, go straight onto Bridge Street (CT 154).*

Proceed across the causeway (a former railroad trestle) separating South Cove from the mouth of the Connecticut River. Take a deep breath of the invigorating salt air blowing off the Sound.

0.9 *At the end of the causeway, turn left onto Nibang Avenue.*

This is the entrance to Fenwick, an exclusive summer colony at the southernmost tip of Old Saybrook. A network of tiny lanes slip past grand cottages where generations of well-to-do Yankee families have spent their summers. The center of the peninsula is a golf course, open to the public in the off-season. Please respect the signs that designate private roads.

1.1 *At the stop sign, proceed straight onto Nibang Avenue.*

1.4 *Bear right onto Neponset Avenue.*

1.6 *Turn left onto Mohegan Avenue.*

This will turn into Agawam Avenue.

1.8 *At the stop sign, turn right onto Fenwick Avenue.*

2.0 *At the stop sign, turn left onto Nibang Avenue.*

2.2 *Turn left onto Maple Avenue (CT 154).*

This dramatic stretch of road hugs the coast and affords sweeping views of Long Island Sound off Knollwood Beach.

3.7 *Turn left onto Cottage Road.*

Cornfield Point is a peninsula crammed with beach cottages presided over by a massive castle with a hard-to-miss red-tile roof.

3.8 *At the stop sign, turn right onto Sea Lane.*

Proceed straight through the next two stop signs. There are several designated overlook areas along Sea Lane, which are worth a stop to catch the view of the coastline.

4.0 *At the next stop sign, turn left onto Hartland Drive.*

4.1 *At the stop sign, go straight, bearing left to get to the castle entrance.*

This fieldstone mansion has had a colorful history since it was built on this bluff in 1906. It's gone from private summer home to boys' school to Prohibition-era bootlegging operation to its cur-

A tranquil cove in Old Saybrook.

rent incarnation as the Castle at Cornfield Point, a charming inn and restaurant.

4.3 At the stop sign, turn left onto Pratt Road.

4.4 At the next stop sign, turn left, then take an immediate right onto Ridge Road.

4.5 At the second stop sign, turn left onto Plum Bank Road (CT 154).

As the road curves to the right it becomes Great Hammock Road. You'll cruise between the cottage-packed shoreline and sweeping expanses of tidal marsh and sea grass.

6.2 At the stop sign, turn right onto Old Boston Post Road.

6.7 At the stop sign, turn right onto Pennywise Lane.

7.0 At this stop sign, turn right onto Main Street (CT 154).

On the corner is the James Gallery, an unusual art gallery/soda fountain where you can get ice cream, pastries, and sandwiches while admiring original maritime art.

7.2 At the traffic light, go straight.

7.7 Turn left onto North Cove Road.

This quiet neighborhood on picturesque North Cove has excellent examples of 18th- and 19th-century homes built for prosperous ship captains and merchants.

8.4 Bear right onto Cromwell Place.

8.8 At the stop sign, turn left onto College Street (CT 154).

8.9 Turn left into Fort Saybrook Monument Park, where the ride ends.

Bicycle Shops

Clarke Cycles, 4 Essex Plaza (CT 154), Essex; 860-767-2405

Saybrook Cycle Works, 210 Main Street, Old Saybrook; 860-388-1534

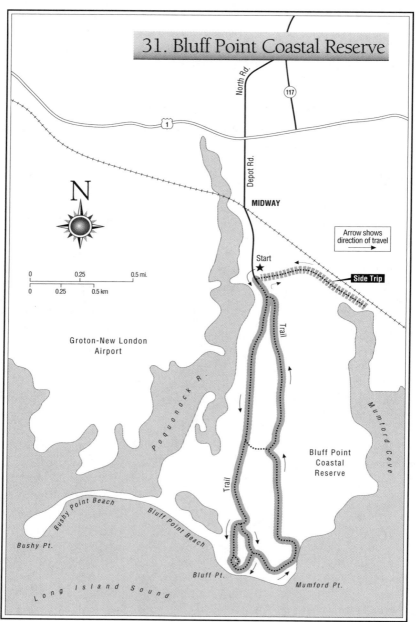

31. Bluff Point Coastal Reserve

North Rd.

117

1

Depot Rd.

MIDWAY

N

0   0.25   0.5 mi.
0   0.25   0.5 km

Arrow shows
direction of travel

Start

Side Trip

Trail

Groton-New London
Airport

Poquonock R.

Mumford Cove

Trail

Bluff Point
Coastal
Reserve

Bushy Point Beach

Bluff Point Beach

Bushy Pt.

Bluff Pt.

Mumford Pt.

Long Island Sound

Paul Woodward, © 2000 The Countryman Press

31
Bluff Point State Park and Coastal Reserve

Distance: *A 4-mile loop; many additional miles of singletrack trails*
Terrain: *Flat, with some short rolling sections*
Difficulty: *Moderate*
Recommended bicycle: *Mountain bike*

Bluff Point State Park and Coastal Reserve in Groton is one of the few remaining pieces of undisturbed coastline in Connecticut. Cyclists, hikers, and equestrians can explore this beautiful 800-acre peninsula of upland hardwoods, sand dunes, wetlands, and beach jutting out into Long Island Sound. The highlights of the state's only coastal preserve, just west of Mystic, are the rocky bluff at the peninsula's tip, a 100-acre tidal salt marsh, and a narrow, 0.5-mile-long sand spit reaching toward Bushy Point, a small rocky island at the tip of the beach.

You can tour the peninsula on an easy 4-mile loop of old, well-worn horse-cart paths, made challenging by areas of loose rock and sand and some short climbs. The route goes past bayberry, beach plum, and seaside goldenrod, which grow wild along the beaches and tidal marshes. Many interesting side trails invite further exploration; some lead right to the shore, while others snake into the peninsula's darker, wooded interior. As you crest the sparsely vegetated rocky bluff the view broadens, and the peninsula abruptly drops some 30 feet below. From this vantage point you can see Watch Hill, Rhode Island, and Fishers Island, New York, on a clear day.

Wildlife is abundant here, which you will likely spot if you ride during the early morning or evening hours. Common terns and piping plovers nest in the dunes, and the forested hills are home to hawks, cottontail rabbits, and even white-tailed deer, which are often seen along the

Long Island Sound as seen from Bluff Point in Groton.

trails and in the thickets and forest edges. The area offers some excellent bird-watching, especially during the summer and fall migrations.

Bluff Point has many prime picnicking sites, the best being on the bluff itself, and a grassy area near the parking lot, with a small trail leading to a point jutting into the Poquonock River. This is a good spot to watch river traffic and small planes taking off from Groton–New London Airport on the opposite shore.

Directions for the Ride

Take I-95 east to exit 88. Follow CT 117 south to US 1 and take it west. At Groton Town Hall, turn left onto Depot Street; continue under the railroad overpass to the gravel parking area. The park is located 2 miles south of the junction of CT 117 and I-95 in Groton.

0.0 *From the parking lot, ride toward the picnic area and pass through the green gate.*

Follow the dirt road from the gate.

0.1 *At the Y in the trail, bear right.*

Growing thickly along the trail are sprawling tangles of bitter-sweet, honeysuckle, greenbriar, and other low-growing shrubs typical of coastal vegetation.

In the early part of the 20th century, there was a community of summer cottages along these dirt roads. In one swift blow, they were ravaged in a 1938 hurricane. The peninsula became a state park in 1975.

1.6 *Follow the small, wood-plank boardwalk on the right to Bluff Point Beach.*

This long, narrow, crushed-shell beach stretches like a crescent along Long Island Sound, ending at Bushy Point. Its small dunes and strong stands of beach grass make it an ideal habitat for gulls, terns, sandpipers, and migrating shorebirds.

1.7 *Just past Bluff Point Beach, bear right at the next side trail to the bluff.*

From here, the trail continues to follow the coastline along Mumford Cove for a short time before veering left into the woods. Despite the thick stands of birch, hickory, and oak, you can often glimpse the sparkling water below to the left as the trail leads to a long, fast descent through the woods along the peninsula's ridge.

On the way down, you'll pass the site of the house built by Connecticut governor John Winthrop, whose family farmed the desolate peninsula in the 18th century. All that remains of the c. 1700 homestead is the rubble of the foundation and stone walls, which you can see from the trail.

4.0 At the next Y in the trail, bear right to return to the parking lot.
At this point, you can begin the loop again and explore some of the side trails within the peninsula. Another option is to return through the green gate and turn immediately right onto the dirt road passing through a picnic area. In about 1 mile, the trail follows railroad tracks (keep a safe distance away from these frequently used tracks). When you see a sign for Palmers Cove at the tracks, look for trails on the right that crisscross a smaller section of the preserve. Swans, scaups, mallards, and other waterfowl are commonly seen in this quiet inlet off Mumford Cove.

Bicycle Shops

Bicycle Barn, 1209 Poquonock Road (US 1), Groton; 860-448-2984

Groton Cyclery, 1360 CT 184, Groton; 860-445-6745

Mystic Cycle Centre, 42 Williams Avenue (US 1), Mystic; 860-572-7433

Terra Cyclery, 154 Williams Street, New London; 860-443-7223

Wayfarer Bicycle, 120 Ocean Avenue (just off US 1), New London; 860-443-8250

32
Stonington

Distance: *28.9 miles*
Terrain: *Flat, with a few rolling hills*
Difficulty: *Moderate*
Recommended bicycle: *Touring/road bike*

The charming fishing village of Stonington is symbolic of everything that is coastal New England. Its rich history of whaling, trading, and exploring stretches back to the early 1600s, when the Pequot Indians set up a fort and traded here, and to 1649, when William Chesebrough and other Englishmen arrived from Plymouth Colony to settle this narrow peninsula reaching into the Atlantic, unprotected by the nearby islands in Long Island Sound.

Water Street is the borough's main avenue of commerce, fronted by stately Greek Revival buildings and other restored 19th-century structures. Prosperous bankers, merchants, and ship owners dwelled in the stately homes lining Main Street. Many other houses here date to the 1700s; namely, the small humble homes of fishermen and craftsmen who lived here at that time.

Pedaling around the peninsula's clean, orderly grid of narrow streets, it's easy to imagine the thriving fishing village of long ago, when sleek clipper ships sailed from Water Street and the young sea captain Nathaniel Palmer left Stonington to discover Antarctica.

In the 19th century, Stonington was a hub for New England's whaling and sealing industries. Today, the borough is home to the state's only active commercial fishing fleet, operating out of the town dock on Pearl Street. The village hosts an annual summertime Blessing of the Fleet in Stonington Harbor. The waters that surround the borough on three sides are dotted with fishing vessels and sailboats.

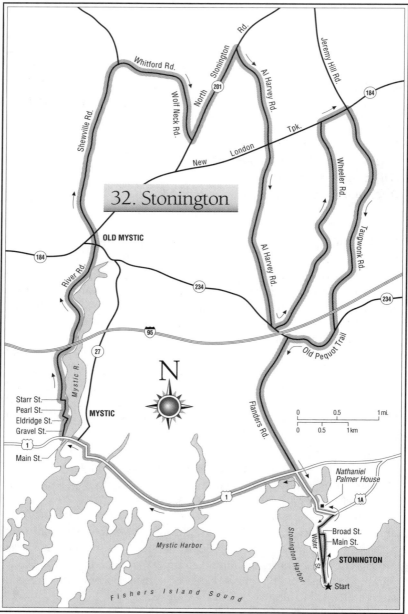

32. Stonington

OLD MYSTIC

MYSTIC

Starr St.
Pearl St.
Eldridge St.
Gravel St.
Main St.

Whitford Rd.

North Stonington Rd.

Al Harvey Rd.

Jeremy Hill Rd.

Wolf Neck Rd.

Shewville Rd.

New   London   Tpk.

Wheeler Rd.

Taugwonk Rd.

River Rd.

Mystic R.

Al Harvey Rd.

Old Pequot Trail

Flanders Rd.

N

0   0.5   1 mi.
0   0.5   1 km

Nathaniel Palmer House

Broad St.
Main St.

Water St.

STONINGTON

★ Start

Stonington Harbor

Mystic Harbor

F i s h e r s   I s l a n d   S o u n d

Paul Woodward, © 2000 The Countryman Press

During the American Revolution and again in the War of 1812, residents fended off the British navy from raiding the harbor, giving Stonington the distinction of being the only port to do this twice. Signs of battle can be found around town, including a marker at Stonington Point, a flag from a battering mast now hanging in the Greek Revival bank on Water Street, a pair of cannons in Cannon Square, and British cannonballs found on stone columns and hitching posts along the village streets.

From Stonington, the ride follows the coves and harbors west along Long Island Sound to the quaint maritime village of Mystic. Some of the world's fastest clipper ships were built in shipyards here along the Mystic River in the 1800s. The village also boasts a magnificent maritime center featuring the country's largest maritime museum, spectacular tall ships, and a re-created 19th-century New England whaling village.

From Mystic, the ride turns away from the coast and meanders through North Stonington's pleasantly rural countryside, which is dotted with old homesteads and laced with the rambling stone walls that gave the town its name.

Directions for the Ride

The ride begins from the parking lot at the tip of the peninsula, next to DuBois Beach at the end of Water Street. Stonington is located off I-95, exit 91, just south of US 1.

For coffee and baked goods, there is no better place in the borough than the Yellow House Coffee & Tea Room at 149 Water Street. During the busy summer season, its lunch menu is expanded with sandwiches named for historic sites around town.

0.0 Ride inland on Water Street.

This is narrow and has two-way traffic, unlike most of Water Street, so use caution. The stone lighthouse at the end of Water Street was the first government-operated lighthouse in Connecticut to protect ships and fishing vessels from the craggy coastline; today, it's the home base of the Stonington Historical Society.

0.2 Turn right at Cannon Square, then immediately go left around the square onto Main Street.

Watch for the 1827 Old Customs House and the handsome 1780 Colonel Amos Palmer House along this street of historic homes.

0.6 Turn left on Broad Street.

0.7 At the stop sign, turn right onto Water Street. Take the bridge over the railroad tracks.

1.0 Turn left on US 1A. Go through the next stop sign.

1.2 At this stop sign, follow US 1A to the right.

The Captain Nathaniel Palmer House (860-535-8445) is just ahead on the right. At the young age of 21, Palmer sailed from Stonington on his 47-foot sloop, *Hero,* and discovered Antarctica. Today, the 16-room Victorian mansion is open to the public and is filled with artifacts of maritime history.

1.8 At the traffic light, turn left onto US 1.

The 2.5-mile stretch along this notoriously busy shoreline route is complemented by a comfortably wide shoulder and pleasing views of the harbors and inlets fringing Long Island Sound.

4.9 Follow US 1 as it curves sharply to the left in Mystic.

5.2 Cross the Mystic River drawbridge.

Use caution on the bridge's metal surface, which could be slippery. An option is to walk your bike on the pedestrian walkway.

On the opposite bank is the heart of downtown Mystic, where boutiques, eateries, and ice cream shops crowd both sides of Main Street.

5.3 Immediately after crossing the drawbridge, turn right onto Gravel Street.

This narrow side street will lead you past charming 18th- and 19th-century homes along the beautiful Mystic River.

5.5 At the stop sign, go straight.

5.7 Turn right onto Pearl Street.

5.9 Turn right onto River Road.

8.3 At the traffic light, go straight. Shortly, you'll reach a stop sign, where you'll turn left onto Shewville Road.

8.4 Continue straight through the traffic light.

The streets in Stonington Borough are lined with well-preserved 18th- and 19th-century homes.

This quiet residential area soon opens to cornfields and the rolling pastures of horse farms.

10.8 Go straight onto Whitford Road.

This narrow ribbon of road passes by the weathered barns and rock-strewn fields of a dairy farm before entering the woods.

11.4 At the stop sign, go straight across Lantern Hill Road onto Wolf Neck Road.

For the next several miles, you'll ride winding country roads past rural homesteads and farms.

12.5 At the stop sign, turn left onto North Stonington Road (CT 201).

13.8 Turn right onto Al Harvey Road.

15.2 At the stop sign, cross New London Turnpike (CT 184).

17.7 At the next stop sign, turn left onto Pequot Trail. Proceed about 100 feet, then turn left onto Wheeler Road.

20.8 At the stop sign, turn right onto CT 184.

21.2 At the blinking traffic light, turn right onto Taugwonk Road.

On this gradual descent you'll pass Stonington Vineyards, makers of award-winning wines, including a popular Seaport Series. The 12-acre vineyard benefits from a maritime microclimate thanks to nearby Long Island Sound. The vineyard and winery (860-535-1222) is open daily and offers tours and tastings.

24.3 At the traffic light, go straight onto Old Pequot Trail. Don't follow the signs you'll see pointing to Stonington Borough.

25.1 Just past the Road Church, turn left onto Flanders Road.

27.0 At the traffic light, cross US 1 and follow signs for Stonington village.

27.8 Turn left onto Trumbull Street.

27.9 Continue straight at the stop sign.

28.0 At the next stop sign, turn right and go over the bridge.

28.9 Return to the parking lot at the tip of Water Street, where the ride ends.

Bicycle Shops

Bicycle Barn, 1209 Poquonock Road (US 1), Groton; 860-448-2984

Groton Cyclery, 1360 CT 184, Groton; 860-445-6745

Mystic Cycle Centre, 42 Williams Avenue (US 1), Mystic; 860-572-7433

Let Backcountry Guides Take You There

Our experienced backcountry authors will lead you to the finest trails, parks, and back roads in the following areas:

50 Hikes Series
50 Hikes in the Adirondacks
50 Hikes in Connecticut
50 Hikes in the Maine Mountains
50 Hikes in Coastal and Southern Maine
50 Hikes in Massachusetts
50 Hikes in Maryland
50 Hikes in Michigan
50 Hikes in the White Mountains
50 More Hikes in New Hampshire
50 Hikes in New Jersey
50 Hikes in Central New York
50 Hikes in Western New York
50 Hikes in the Mountains of North Carolina
50 Hikes in Ohio
50 Hikes in Eastern Pennsylvania
50 Hikes in Central Pennsylvania
50 Hikes in Western Pennsylvania
50 Hikes in the Tennessee Mountains
50 Hikes in Vermont
50 Hikes in Northern Virginia

Walks and Rambles Series
Walks and Rambles on Cape Cod and the Islands
Walks and Rambles on the Delmarva Peninsula
Walks and Rambles in the Western Hudson Valley
Walks and Rambles on Long Island
Walks and Rambles in Ohio's Western Reserve
Walks and Rambles in Rhode Island
Walks and Rambles in and around St. Louis

25 Bicycle Tours Series
25 Bicycle Tours in the Adirondacks
25 Bicycle Tours on Delmarva
25 Bicycle Tours in Savannah and the Carolina Low Country
25 Bicycle Tours in Maine
25 Bicycle Tours in Maryland
25 Bicycle Tours in the Twin Cities and Southeastern Minnesota
30 Bicycle Tours in New Jersey
30 Bicycle Tours in the Finger Lakes Region
25 Bicycle Tours in the Hudson Valley
25 Bicycle Tours in Maryland
25 Bicycle Tours in Ohio's Western Reserve
25 Bicycle Tours in the Texas Hill Country and West Texas
25 Bicycle Tours in Vermont
25 Bicycle Tours in and around Washington, D.C.
30 Bicycle Tours in Wisconsin
25 Mountain Bike Tours in the Adirondacks
25 Mountain Bike Tours in the Hudson Valley
25 Mountain Bike Tours in Massachusetts
25 Mountain Bike Tours in New Jersey
Backroad Bicycling on Cape Cod, Martha's Vineyard, and Nantucket
Backroad Bicycling in Eastern Pennsylvania
The Mountain Biker's Guide to Ski Resorts

Bicycling America's National Parks Series
Bicycling America's National Parks: Arizona & New Mexico
Bicycling America's National Parks: California
Bicycling America's National Parks: Oregon & Washington
Bicycling America's National Parks: Utah & Colorado

We offer many more books on hiking, fly-fishing, travel, nature, and other subjects. Our books are available at bookstores and outdoor stores everywhere. For more information or a free catalog, please call 1-800-245-4151 or write to us at The Countryman Press, P.O. Box 748, Woodstock, Vermont 05091. You can find us on the Internet at www.countrymanpress.com.